The Homecoming

The Homecoming

The Lionesses
and Beyond

Jane Purdon

FOOTBALL
SHORTS

**FOOTBALL
SHORTS**

Series curator Ian Ridley

First published by Pitch Publishing
and Floodlit Dreams, 2023

Pitch Publishing
9 Donnington Park,
85 Birdham Road,
Chichester,
West Sussex,
PO20 7AJ
www.pitchpublishing.co.uk
info@pitchpublishing.co.uk

A CIP catalogue record is available for this book
from the British Library.

ISBN 978 1 80150 484 3

Back cover picture of Jane Purdon by Lynne Cameron

Typesetting and origination by Pitch Publishing

Printed and bound in Great Britain by TJ Books, Padstow

For Mum, Dad, and AH

ACKNOWLEDGEMENTS

I OWE a huge debt of thanks to many people for their help with this book. First, I must say thank you to Ian Ridley not just for the idea of the book, but for his relentless work to get more women's writing about football published, and for his tireless support throughout the writing process.

To produce a book takes a village, and my thanks also go to all at Pitch Publishing and Floodlit Dreams, and to editor Charlotte Atyeo, cover designer Duncan Olner and Football Shorts website creator Alex Ridley.

Next up are those who gave of their time so generously to discuss the issues in this book or otherwise help me: Alice Ritson, Anita Abayomi, Annabel Ritson, Ben Wright, Eartha Pond, Eden Bailey, Edleen John, Gareth Prosser, Helen Foster,

Helen Fram, Helen Wright, Kelly Simmons, Laura Youngson, Lewis Gray, Louise Matthews, Malcolm Fram, Mark Harrison, Mary Phillip, Matt M, Monique Choudhuri, Nadine Kessler, Paul Ritson, Pontus Alveryd, Sally-Anne Betts, Valerie Heron and Yvonne Harrison.

Thanks also to Carly Perry, Aiden J. Chauntry and Francesca Champ for their June 2022 article in *Science and Medicine in Football* on mental ill-health in elite female footballers.

There is a warm and wonderful community of football fans, players, workers, writers, podcasters and women's football addicts on social media who over the years have informed me, made me laugh and made me cry. Thank you – and may we continue to be delighted eyewitnesses to the growth of the women's game.

Huge thanks to all my colleagues, past and present, at Women in Football and PGAAC. Every day you work tirelessly to make football better, and the game owes all of you an enormous debt.

Thanks also to all at my lovely new football set-up: it's a joy to play with you, it's a joy to get to know you, it's a joy to be part of the revolution that has brought recreational football for older women to our town.

My gratitude also goes to the staff and my fellow students on my creative writing degree courses, and in particular to my tutors Lizzi Linklater at the University of York and Jennifer Nansubuga Makumbi and Oliver Harris at Manchester Metropolitan University. As Jill Scott said about the Euros trophy, your hands are on this too.

And most importantly my thanks and my love go to AH. For everything. For absolutely everything, not least for all the love, tea and support from the first day when I thought I might just have a go at writing.

1

THERE'S A bench on the way to the supermarket from our house. It has a view down to the pedestrian level crossing over the little branch line where one train ambles up and back all day, 20 minutes from terminus to terminus. If you're on the bench when the train approaches the level crossing, you'll hear it hoot to warn pedestrians before you see it. And then it grumbles into view and chugs slowly over the crossing.

But mostly when you sit on the bench, you just see the railway line, and maybe the odd person walking or cycling over the crossing. If it's July, you see a patch of long grass that the council doesn't mow any more, and you see trees, and you hear bird song and the odd car on the road behind you. I sometimes take myself away to sit on the

bench for a bit of calm, a bit of forest bathing –
or the closest to it that the English suburbs can
muster: the unmown grass, the stand of sycamores
bordered by scrub of blackthorn and hawthorn,
and the singing of sparrows and blackbirds in the
treetops.

I went to sit there for a spell on Saturday 30 July
2022 because I was experiencing mental overload.

Over the previous three weeks, during one
of the hottest English summers on record, the
UEFA Women's Euros had played out in Brentford,
Wigan, Sheffield, Manchester, Rotherham, Milton
Keynes, Southampton and Brighton. England – the
Lionesses – had battled and danced their way past
all opposition and the next day would see them take
on Germany in the showpiece final at Wembley. It
was really getting to me.

I'd been to Wembley finals before. I'd been to
one only two months previously when Sunderland
had beaten Wycombe Wanderers in the League
One play-off final. I'd supported Sunderland since
childhood but I'd been disenchanted with the
men's team over recent years. However, with new

ownership and new leadership, they had beaten Wycombe in that all-important Wembley game. It felt like they were finally beginning to take their first steps back into the light. But what was at stake in that game in May was the future of two clubs. As I sat on the bench that Saturday, I realised that what was at stake at Wembley the next day was the future of an entire sport.

The final represented the opportunity for the dreams that many of us had held for decades to become reality. If the Lionesses won, women's and girls' football in England would be turbo-charged to kick on to a whole new reality, one where it would never again be mocked or marginalised.

Important football finals are moments of definition. They are both end points and beginnings. The stories of all the people who've worked hard to get a team to a final draw together to a single point, like the perspective lines in a Renaissance painting converging to take the eye and the mind to a central area of focus. And then at the final whistle, all these lines split off and dance and dazzle their way into the future.

On Friday 29 July, the day before I sat on the bench, The FA had put up Jill Scott for the Lionesses' last media conference. At 35 years old, Jill had been an England stalwart for over a decade. She played in the elite game before it was fully professional and, like me, she was an eyewitness to the rise and rise of women's football. Also like me, she was in a contemplative mood, her thoughts turning to all those who'd worked hard without thanks, including 'volunteers that went and helped out their local girls' teams, the ones that are still doing it, the ones that love the game.' Then she looked around the room and said, 'I see reporters in here and I've seen them in here for the past 16 years and they do it for the love of the game. So I hope everybody knows that on Sunday if we are to lift that trophy, they've all got their hand on it as well.' Jill knew. She knew there were myriad individual stories – about effort, about dreaming even when hurt, about keeping going, and most of all about damn hard work – that had brought us to this point.

So there I was on the bench after three weeks of the drama, joy, anxiety, tears, shredded nerves and ecstasy provided by the Lionesses' journey through these Euros. As I sat there, I felt my own personal history in the game crashing down on me. Memories and moments kept flooding in, hitting me with force. I made a conscious decision to think about my journey in the game, hoping that rehearsing it all now might stop me being overwhelmed by it the next day.

I went back to my seven-year-old self, a young girl growing up in Sunderland in the 1972/73 season in a state of ignorance of what football was. It was something men did. My father and brother went to watch football on Saturday afternoons. My brother and his friends would be out all day playing football. Nothing was ever said about why football was not for girls; it was just assumed and accepted. Yet three football-related things were to happen in close succession around that time and they were to profoundly change my life. I wasn't to know about two of them for many years, but the third happened in May 1973 and it turned out to be my ur-football moment.

Although not Sunderland natives, my family had lived there since Dad's work as a naval architect brought us over from Merseyside when I was three. Dad immediately started going to watch Sunderland. At that time, they were languishing at the bottom of the table and were shortly to be relegated to the old Second Division, having once been one of the greats. No one expected much of them, but that season Sunderland's Ian Porterfield scored the only goal of the 1973 FA Cup Final, with the result that Sunderland – the rank outsiders – beat Leeds United, the team who in recent years had swept all before them.

I was seven, and I watched the final at home in Sunderland with my mum (my dad and brother had gone to Wembley). When I saw Porterfield score on TV I had a physical sensation of falling. It was as if a chasm opened and I tumbled down into it, never to climb back out. That chasm was love, and from exactly 3.32pm on 5 May 1973 I've been a football fan and, as we say in County Durham, Sunderland Till I Die.

My father was a man of his times and had never thought his daughter would want to watch football, but he was also happy enough to indulge his kids in whatever they wanted to do, as long as it wouldn't kill them. When I asked if I could start going to watch Sunderland too, he said 'yes' immediately and without judgement. I'll be grateful for ever. My first steps in my lifelong journey with football were taken.

Looking back, I bemoan that the first day of my Sunderland support was also the greatest. There were to be no more Wembley trips or success of any kind for many years, but I spent every second Saturday happily at Roker Park, comfortable and content in the company of the menfolk in my life. Roker Park was a dump. It was a very romantic dump, but it was a dump. We stood in the uncovered Roker End, often in the corner next to the iron railings that separated it from the Clock Stand. The railings were as high as I was and they had an icy, acidic smell. There were midwinter matches when an easterly wind would whip in glacial showers from the North Sea. But I always felt warm.

This was both a physical warmth from the proximity of bodies around us and a psychological warmth, a safety. And it has to be said: the reason I felt so psychologically safe was because I was surrounded by men. Even though I never spotted another young girl, and few adult women, never once did I feel this was an alien environment. I was tolerated, welcomed even. In this place, we were all equal, united as a family by our love of Sunderland AFC. And yet this was a place where men were to be found and women, largely, were not. I could not understand this. Football was wonderful: it was dramatic, it was exciting, it was comradely. Why didn't everyone do it? Well, welcome to the patriarchy, baby girl.

We watched men's football at Roker Park, of course. I cannot remember ever in my childhood being aware that such a thing as women's football existed. But exist it did, albeit as a shadow of its former self. It had been hugely popular as a spectator sport during and immediately after the First World War. In the early 1920s The FA – the national governing body for the game – suppressed women's football by stopping it being played on grounds belonging to FA-affiliated clubs. This had the desired effect, and a sport that had attracted crowds of tens of thousands was bullied into utter retreat.

It didn't die completely but it wasn't a proper, organised thing for many more years. What's more, the decades-long suppression of the game by The FA enabled a toxic culture to build up whereby any female involvement in the game was ridiculed and abused. In the junior school playground, I wasn't believed when I said I'd been at Roker Park the previous Saturday. I had to run through the team and the key moments of the match before there'd be a reluctant shrug of acceptance. It was an early lesson that women often have to work harder to prove themselves.

I mentioned that there were two other things that happened around this time. First, The FA lifted the ban on women playing at FA-affiliated grounds almost 50 long years after imposing it. A new age began – but for your average English primary schoolgirl of the time, it began with a whimper. Was there a rush to ensure girls and women could play? No.

The second thing happened in June 1972 on the other side of the Atlantic, and I wasn't to find out about it for many years.

For now, my young football life focused on going to games with Dad and my brother. But there came a rupture of the worst kind. My father was diagnosed with Motor Neurone Disease when I was 11. Lots of things stopped, including the three of us going to watch football. For two years I watched my hero die a little bit more each day. In June 1979, he went to Matfen Hall in Northumberland, then a care home, to give my mother, his full-time carer, some respite. The ambulance collected him on the Monday. He died on the Tuesday.

It was the start of a world that was different, and I wasn't given a map to navigate it. My mother fell ill with what was then called a nervous breakdown. She eventually recovered, but I effectively had to self-parent during my early teens. School saved me to an extent. At a time when my world was out of control, I found I could control studying. It never felt like work – rather, I enjoyed it enormously. What's more, I was good at it and got good results. But I was stumbling about in pain, my excellent school results misguidedly reassuring every responsible adult that I was 'fine' and 'coming through it well'.

When bereavement is breaking you, you'll try anything. One Saturday when I was about 15, I was meandering around the house, broken and lonely. Mum was having a bad day and not up to doing anything. I picked up the paper and saw that Sunderland were playing at home. *What the hell*, I thought, and I set off.

The direct walk to Roker Park from our house took about 40 minutes. The indirect way, which took about an hour, is one of the most beautiful walks I know. It starts with a climb up to the top of Cleadon Hills, a magnesian limestone escarpment and a landscape not quite like any other in England. The escarpment's topped with soft grass where harebells and cowslips nod, while overhead the sky rings with lark song. From the top, the whole of God's great North-East of England opens out before you: 30-odd miles to the south, the North Yorkshire Moors; far in the north, the Cheviots; in between, the great river plains of Tyne, Wear and Tees and the cities they support. And to the east – the sea.

It's to the sea that I'd head, following the path to Whitburn, an ancient and delightful coastal village, typical of County Durham villages with its Front Street of stone cottages and its huge village green. From here, the walk was along the golden mile of beach that so inspired the painter L.S. Lowry. At the farthest end of the beach, you'd cut up through the original Roker Park, a Victorian pleasure ground with bandstand, bowling greens and boating lake. Then you'd come out of the park, round a corner and see the floodlights of the football ground. Floodlights mounted on four tall pylons, one at each corner of the ground, have now all but disappeared, but back then they were a familiar and comforting part of every cityscape.

The first sight of the Roker Park floodlights on matchday always gave me a tug of excitement, on this day as much as on any other. I went in the Roker End, where we'd always gone. I can't remember the match or the score but I remember it was a sunny day late in the season and that I looked around trying to find Dad. He wasn't entirely absent: call it memory, call it presence, call it a ghost, but something of him was there.

Other things were still most definitely and concretely there: the crowd of mostly men and their intense focus – sometimes agonised, sometimes ecstatic – on the match being played out before them; the tinny tannoy; the smell of the iron railings, the cigarettes being smoked all around, and a freshness blowing in from the sea while gulls cried overhead. I soon found I was engrossed in the match, but most of all I had overwhelming feelings of belonging and of safety – the epitome of being at home.

Over the next few years, I became something of a Roker regular again. Not every match, sometimes just the odd match, and always alone, football fandom for girls still being something of a minority pursuit. Eventually another rupture with Sunderland AFC came, this time because Cambridge beckoned when I left school.

Before Cambridge there was a trip to study at an American boarding school for six months as a result of being awarded an English-Speaking Union scholarship. The USA was further than I had ever travelled and the prospect of the trip was both exhilarating and daunting. Talking to some Americans in the London hotel where my mother and I stayed the night before my flight from Heathrow, we told them the school was called Choate Rosemary Hall. The Americans went silent. Mum and I side-eyed each other. Eventually, the American lady said, 'You do know that's the school John F. Kennedy went to?' No, we had no idea. We knew nothing about this school. It was 1985, the internet was ten years away, and we'd had no means of finding out. And before we could digest properly what we'd just learned, I was away on the flight to New York.

What an adventure. Choate Rosemary Hall was the epitome of privileged secondary education in the USA and I had never seen anything like it. I had never met people from the backgrounds some of these people were from: fabulously, globally wealthy. Most of them tended to wear it fairly lightly. You can tell what class a British person wants you to think they are from the way they speak but also from other markers such as how they dress. The same is true of Americans but not to the same extent.

I found an open-hearted, can-do approach to life and a generosity of spirit that made the British seem crabbed. This generosity expressed itself in myriad kindnesses to me from my schoolmates and their families, and I came to have the deepest respect for the United States. Not everything was perfect: I remember being staggered by some of the poverty I saw outside the ivied precincts of Choate, and when I travelled to some of the big cities I remember being shocked by the extent to which poor areas correlated to Black areas.

But back in the ivied precincts of Choate, I saw that it had better sports facilities than many British universities. Every sport was played and for a lot of the students and faculty sport was an obsession. 'Ah, you British, it must be wonderful to play your tennis on grass,' one teacher said to me. *Mate*, I thought, *I'm from a shipbuilding family in Sunderland – yes, a middle-class one, but still.*

But Choate was to blow my brain for footballing reasons: it had a girls' soccer team. Not only that, but the team played in a well-established league. I was astounded. *How did ... how come ... there's girls playing football? And it's normal? Nobody thinks they're weird?* Then one day the girls' soccer coach came up to me and said, 'Hey, you're British, I guess you play. Do you fancy a try-out?'

How on earth could this be? The answer was that thing that had happened in the USA in June 1972. It was a piece of legislation called Title IX, which banned discrimination in any education programmes receiving federal assistance. It had the effect of huge new funding streams becoming available to girls' and women's school and college sport. All that money needed something to spend itself on and along came soccer, as our American friends call it. Without all the ridiculous cultural baggage about the game's unsuitability for females that burdened it in its home country, it met its American destiny. And so here I was, 13 years after Title IX was enacted, being asked to play football. I was being asked to play football!

CHAPTER 1

I had to look at the coach and reply, 'I'm terribly sorry, but I've never kicked a ball.'

Rage entered my soul. How come I had never kicked a ball? Why had my country let me down in this way? Back home in Britain, we talked of football as our national sport but this was nonsense if only half the population could play. I brought a lot of things home from my six months in America, and this deep anger with my country was one of the most important. I felt that in denying me football, it had let me down. It was holding me back.

But I wasn't a child any more. There was something I could do about it. When I started at Clare College, Cambridge in the autumn of 1985, despite having still never kicked a ball, I set up Clare's first-ever women's football team in its 600 years of history. Thus a little rivulet of the huge tide of change that was Title IX flowed back to old England. I like to think the college's 14th-century founder, Lady Elizabeth de Clare, wouldn't entirely have disapproved.

I got the team together for our first match against one of the other colleges by cajoling people in the bar. No one had played before and everyone was a bit scared. 'Oh you won't want me, I'll be no good,' said almost all of them, but somehow I persuaded 11 players to rock up for the game. I think we lost 10-0, but each one of us came off the pitch saying, 'That was wonderful, when's the next game?'

We lost the next game about 6-0, but things began to improve. After one match we were down in the college bar, high as kites. 'Oh, did you win?' asked one of the blokes. 'No, we lost 2-0!' I replied. It was a defeat, but it felt like a proper football score, not a netball score. We played on. Eventually we started scoring goals – and oh, the ecstasy!

How was all this received in Clare College? Just fine. In 1972 it had become one of the first three all-male colleges to admit women students. It was widely seen as liberal and progressive. The general ambience around the place was that academic life was important, but outside that nobody was too bothered what you did, although it was nice if you did it well.

CHAPTER 1

There are things that I've experienced for the first time as an adult that have given me a sense of utter wonder, things that younger generations will take for granted. Having a real-time email conversation with someone in Chile. Seeing red kites, the glorious bird of prey reintroduced at the turn of the century, soaring in English skies. And playing football.

My god, what a revelation it was. Football is quite simply the greatest and most enjoyable game it is possible to play. It demands everything of the athlete: ideally you have to be fit, fast and flexible; you have to be skilful as an individual but you also have to play as a team. It's a tactical game that makes you think, but it isn't bogged down by strategy. Every part of you – mind and body – is exercised, worked out and brought alive. I absolutely loved it. It felt so freeing and glorious to charge around a pitch in the sharp, damp, English autumn air. Then there was the basic, atavistic pleasure of one's relationship with the ball: feeling its responses to your touch and beginning to understand how to control it. After a while came the enormous pleasure when it began to click with my team-mates – passing a ball into space for them to run on to, or being the last woman in defence before the keeper and getting in the vital tackle.

There was something else too, something that is perhaps unique to women: suddenly, and for the first time in my life, I had permission to be aggressive. For many young women of my generation, even though feminism had done so much to change the world, any sign of being combative or sometimes even just assertive would be squashed flat. Aggression (properly used, within the Laws of the Game) isn't just desirable in football, it's essential. You're face to face with opponents. You can't walk away. Allowing my assertiveness to flow on the football pitch was one of the greatest revelations I have ever experienced.

I really, really wasn't very good. That's not false modesty, it's a cool-headed self-assessment. But I kept playing after Cambridge, first as a post-grad at Northumbria University and then in the law firm where I worked as a trainee solicitor. In both these places I set up teams. As a mediocre female player in the early 1990s, it was the only way to play. Each time I had that experience of rounding up a group of women who, bar one or two exceptions, hadn't played before. Each time I asked someone, the answer would invariably be the same as I'd got at Cambridge: 'You won't want me, I won't be very good.' It was rare that a woman simply said, 'Yes.' But for those who said I wouldn't want them, I also saw the shine in their eyes that suggested they really, really wanted to give it a go but couldn't allow themselves to say so. I'd persuade, pressure, cajole and reassure, and eventually get my teams together. And every time they came off the pitch smiling and wanting to play again.

In the country at large, women's football was at long last beginning to be a thing again. A Women's Football Association had been established, and by the mid-1980s there was an England team. When I moved to London after university, there was an embryonic set-up under the auspices of Arsenal FC. I even went along to one of its training sessions but I was totally outclassed.

Reactions to the fact that I played football fell along a spectrum. Some people, particularly at Cambridge and in the world of fanzines and fan culture in which I grew increasingly involved, were extremely supportive. Others expressed amused curiosity and slight disbelief. It was always, always a talking point. I came to expect it to be the one thing that would be picked out of my CV for discussion at job interviews. And then there was the downright hostility, invariably accompanied by one or both of the Two Hostile Questions. Hostile Question Number One was: are you all lesbians? Hostile Question Number Two was: do you all swap shirts at the end? (But hey, it's just banter, right?)

Throughout my twenties there was still Sunderland AFC. I went to see them whenever I could. In my final year at Cambridge, there was joy as manager Denis Smith lifted the club out of the old Third Division. His tenure brought some good players in, and it began to be a real pleasure to go and see them. I chose Northumbria University for post-grad so that I could get a season ticket at Roker Park. Sunderland's fortunes were mixed, but in

CHAPTER 1

1992 – the year I took my Law Society final exams – they got to the FA Cup Final for the first time since 1973. OK, we lost, but what a season to have a season ticket. The quarter-final replay against Chelsea at Roker Park is a game that those who were there still talk about. I wasn't to experience a game like it for intensity, anxiety and emotion until 31 July 2022.

* * *

My football team was on the up and I was playing (albeit intermittently and only when I could be bothered to set a team up). One evening an idea came to me in a flash when I was having dinner with my family: 'I'm going to set up a fanzine about women in football.' That was it. No brainstorming, no concept designing, no consultations, no thinking about it. I knew immediately that it was a great idea. Thus 'Born Kicking', my contribution to the cutting edge of 1990s football subculture, was born. It badged itself as the fanzine for women who loved football, whether as players or fans and, if as fans, whether of the male or female game. It ran for four issues, it sold a few hundred copies, it barely covered its costs, and I had to end it because I couldn't run it and do those wretched Law Society final exams and I couldn't find anyone to take it over. But while I ran it, it was a laugh and it got me a bit of prominence as women who knew anything about football were thin on the ground. In later years, I just thought of it as this daft studenty thing I once did and I kind of forgot about it.

I recently reread it for the first time in thirty years. Now, I'm pretty sure it was the first football fanzine in the world for women in football. It was scrappy, it was homemade, you can see the Tippex lines on its photocopied pages, but I wouldn't change one word of Issue One's opening editorial, written in September 1990:

Football is the People's Game. This is both a truth and a truism. A truth, because without doubt football is as an intrinsic and important part of our everyday British culture as the royal family, the pub and the double-decker bus. A truism, because it's a phrase that people glibly trot out without really thinking what it means. Another often heard cliché is 'football is a man's game'. These two statements cannot exist side by side. We believe that football is genuinely and fundamentally by the people and for the people, *all* the people, women as much as men.

I'm now partly proud of 'Born Kicking', partly mortally embarrassed by it. I'm proud of setting out the stall for women in football, for making the case that it ought to be our game too. I'm proud that, among other articles, I interviewed Linda Whitehead (secretary of the Women's Football Association), Martin Regan (England manager), and Kerry Davies (who played for England and semi-professionally in Italy). I'm proud and exceptionally grateful that many other women, and some men, contributed enthusiastically by writing articles and creating artwork, and I thank them again, after all this time, from the bottom of my heart. I'm proud that 'Born Kicking' had a regular 'What the Sexists Say' feature (step up Brian Glanville: 'Women's football is a game that should only be played by consenting adults in private' – Brian, I'm proud that we named and shamed you).

But I'm also embarrassed by some of it, such as the kicking I gave the football bodies, particularly The FA. Some of my writing was naive and uninformed. Having said that, some of what I called for then is as relevant now. Spend money, I argued, on 'the provision of basic things like coaches and pitches'. And then there was this about the new elite national league that was due to start in 1991:

> The question arises of how [the national league] is going to be paid for. The Women's Football Association has limited resources and cannot be expected to fund it all itself, and at the moment is trying to look round for some kind of blue-chip sugar daddy to foot the bill. Where is Barclays now?

In case you don't know, Barclays have been the sponsor of the WSL since 2019 and of Women in Football – the organisation that exists to support, celebrate and champion every woman in the game and of which I was CEO for three years – for many years. In 1991, I was the first person to call on Barclays to sponsor the national women's football league, and here we are.

Mystic Jane didn't stop there. I wrote an article for *When Saturday Comes* in November 1992, and said this:

> The real issue is to get women's football properly publicised, funded and appreciated. The England women's team winning the European Championship – now that is not a fairy tale, it could just happen.'

There you have it: in 1992 I said that the England women's football team could win the Euros.

I sometimes wonder what would have happened if I'd stuck with my work to advocate for women's football, and for women to have their rightful place in football, in the early 1990s. I wonder if my life would have been different. What is striking is that I went off and did other things only to come back years later to where I'd started. But the hard fact was that back then, in my mid-twenties, I couldn't see my way to making a living from advocacy for women in football. It was time for some proper adulting.

After my law exams, I moved back to London to do the hard on-the-job graft necessary to become a fully qualified lawyer. Two years later I achieved my goal and was at long last able to call myself a solicitor. After qualification, I specialised in commercial property disputes. In 1998 my mother died. Broken again, I took time out from my career. When my head and heart began to recover, I didn't really fancy going back to the world of commercial property disputes, so I joined the government legal service. I ended up prosecuting drug smugglers for HM Customs and I bloody loved it. *That's me sorted*, I thought. I couldn't see myself ever leaving. I didn't play football any more (at the turn of the millennium it still wasn't widely available on a recreational level for women), but I still went to see Sunderland when I could.

I honestly thought I'd had my football years and that my continuing football involvement would be only as a fan. But one Sunday in early 2001, a friend rang me and said there was a job in the *Sunday Times* that 'had my name on it'. My beloved Sunderland AFC were looking for a club secretary, 'possibly someone with a legal background'. I pointed out to my friend that I prosecuted drug smugglers, legal experience that would be of little relevance to a Premier League football club (as Sunderland at that time were). 'Just apply,' she said. She was to say it again every day for the next week until I caved under the pressure and sent an application off. I thought I might get a tour of the Stadium of Light, the ground the club had moved to from Roker Park in 1997, and a few dinner-party stories out of it. They gave me the job. I'm still a bit taken aback now.

I was club secretary at Sunderland AFC for four years, working with three managers (Peter Reid,

Howard Wilkinson and Mick McCarthy) under chairman Sir Bob Murray. 'I like having women in my leadership team,' Bob said to me early in my time at the club, 'they bring something different to it.' He meant it. He promoted and supported women in senior positions. It was the strongest affirmation of gender equality and inclusion in the workplace that anyone had ever said to me – and it was said right here in football.

Those four years were eventful and included a relegation from the Premier League in 2003. As I watched dozens of club staff being made redundant at the end of that relegation season, I learned quickly that working in football is not all stardust and sunshine. It's a point I'm always keen to make now to the rooms of fresh-faced students listening to the lectures I give on football business courses. But of course there were good times too. There is nothing quite like working at a football club, particularly if you work at the training ground, as I did. There is a unique spirit and culture in football training grounds, and some of the best humour you'll encounter. My gender was never,

ever an issue with any of the men I worked with. I was given plenty of space to learn the ropes of being a football lawyer and to develop the role of being the club's first-ever in-house solicitor. I got to grips with drafting players' contracts and transfer agreements, dealing with disputes with other clubs, putting together the club's arguments to appeal red cards or for compensation hearings in respect of young players.

And my career at Sunderland ended on a high: in 2005 we were promoted back to the Premier League under Mick McCarthy and my last day of employment was spent following the open-topped team bus parading the trophy round the streets of Sunderland.

The next day I set off for London with my cat – shades of Dick Whittington. The day after that, I started work at the Premier League. It was a tough decision to leave Sunderland but the pull of joining the biggest and best league in the world was too much. My initial role there involved checking all player contracts and transfer agreements and giving the Premier League's all-important tick that would allow a player to be registered for a club. I was also tasked with looking after the Premier League's rule book – the legally binding regulations that governed every aspect of clubs' business and operations. Bizarrely, in my early years I also used to do the fixture list.

My career as a football regulatory lawyer grew as the Premier League itself grew. As more and more money came into the game, there was a need for more and more regulation to control it. I rose to become the Premier League's first-ever director of governance as the rule book grew in complexity. We introduced new rules concerning club profitability and sustainability, who could and could not own a club, and the checks the Premier League would undertake on new owners.

Perhaps the achievement I'm most proud of was drafting the Youth Development Rules, which gave effect to the Elite Player Performance Plan. Now ten years old, the EPPP was a hugely ambitious blueprint designed and written by youth-development experts from across the game. Its ambition was to develop a world-leading academy system and produce more homegrown elite male players. It was a revolution in how football looked after and developed its young talent. My role was to take the vast technical content developed by the experts and turn it into clear, legally binding rules.

But by 2015 I was seeking a new challenge. I took a sideways move to UK Sport. This was yet another moment in my life when I thought, with some wistfulness, that I'd left football. However, there were many upsides. I was working with the British Olympic and Paralympic governing bodies and it was fascinating to get to know other sports. They each have their own culture, their own quirks, their own way of doing things. My main focus was to ensure that the national governing bodies of sport had excellent corporate governance. To me, this seemed only fair in return for the hundreds of millions of pounds they received from the British lottery ticket buyer and the British taxpayer. Jointly with Sport England we wrote something called 'The Code for Sports Governance' and, while I know the topic of sports governance will seem esoteric to most sport fans, it's another of the achievements in my career I'm exceptionally proud of.

And I hadn't really left football. I was still going to see Sunderland when I could, and over the previous 15 years I'd added a new element to my football fandom. I first went to see an England women's game in 1990, in my 'Born Kicking' days, when they played a 0-0 draw against Finland at Brentford's Griffin Park. My moving to Newcastle for post-grad, then working hard as a lawyer, then moving back to Sunderland to work at the football club meant I was less able to go to England women's games. But I started going again around 2009, and I was incredibly impressed by what I saw. It made me suggest to my partner that we go to the Women's World Cup, taking place in Germany in 2011. 'Come and see them first,' I said to him. We went to a friendly against the USA, then the top-ranked nation in the world, at Leyton Orient. There were about 6,000 spectators there, most of them children. Against all expectations, England took the Americans apart and won 2-1. When we were walking out of the ground, I turned to my partner and said, 'Forget you're talking to Mary bloody Wollstonecraft here, tell me what you honestly thought.' 'That,' he said, 'is the best performance by a team in an England shirt that I've seen in two decades. We're going to Germany.'

It was the first of our 'football holidays': two wonderful weeks exploring the 'real' Germany from Wolfsburg to Dresden to Augsburg. We couldn't make it to the 2015 World Cup four years later due to work commitments, but in 2019 we followed England's group stage games in France. We loved these tournaments: you got to see the country and you got to watch some brilliant football. Women's World Cups are big enough to feel like proper sporting events, but no one chucks chairs in town squares or sings songs about the IRA.

Part of the joy of following the national team around a country is that the itinerary is dictated for you. Nobody probably chooses to holiday in Wolfsburg, home of Volkswagen, but in 2011 we got to see and understand the industrial-powerhouse heart of Germany. We went to Dresden for the next match, where I was overwhelmed at the sight of the rebuilt Frauenkirche, bombed to rubble in the war with only a couple of square metres of wall left standing. Rebuilt and reconsecrated only six years before our visit, it stood fresh, bright and shining. When we walked in, a choir was singing Bach and I cried like a child. Then it was south to Augsburg, where England beat the eventual winners, Japan. The Lionesses had topped their group and that night we were invited by The FA's Rachel Pavlou – then and now a stalwart of The FA's women's football set-up – to the team hotel. I had bought the official FIFA poster at the match, and it was passed round the bar, with manager Hope Powell and all the players and the technical staff signing it. It still hangs on my wall, its signatures and lager stains reminding me of one magical night in southern Germany.

Eight years later we travelled to Nice for England's opener against Scotland in the 2019 Women's World Cup. I had always thought that Nice would be a marvellously glamorous place, but I found it to be rather like Eastbourne. Which is fine, I like Eastbourne. After the match, we meandered north by train, spending a couple of days in Lyon, arguably the spiritual home of French women's football. Then it was northwards again to Le Havre for the Lionesses' game against Argentina. The port city of Le Havre was another match venue that was not an obvious holiday destination, but it's a port city with UNESCO World Heritage status for its unique post-war rebuilding. We bookended the match with a stay on Normandy's wonderful coast and visits into the Pays d'Auge – just like the Weald of Kent only with slightly fewer people and slightly better food.

So, sure, we got to see some interesting places, but at the heart of our football travels was our belief in this England team. It was full of world-class talent. My partner's verdict from the first time he had seen them continued to hold good for the next 11 years.

There was an extra attraction for us County Durham people. We Mackems have had our own Golden Generation. Six of the England players who started the 2019 World Cup semi-final against the USA were born or brought up in the North-East or North Yorkshire. All six spent their teenage football years, or a considerable chunk of them, in the Sunderland AFC set-up. Our club had made perhaps the most outstanding contribution to the elite women's game in England ever made by any club. The six included four of the greatest players, of either gender, that this country has ever produced: Steph Houghton, Lucy Bronze, Beth Mead and Jill Scott. As a woman from Wearside, it meant the world to see these women grace the top tournaments of football for so many years.

Our football holidays had also made us eyewitnesses to the growth of interest in the women's game. In 2011, little of the Women's World Cup was shown on television in the UK. In fact, when it comes to television, one of the world-changing events was not from women's football but from women's hockey. On Friday 19 August 2016, the gold-medal women's hockey match at the Rio Olympics between Team GB and the Netherlands was televised live. It overran. That happens, but here's the thing: it delayed the broadcast of BBC One's *News at Ten*. This is a BBC scheduling pillar that nothing shall shake – and yet here was a women's sporting event grabbing its airtime.

For me, this was a pivotal moment. Barbara Slater is the director of sport at the BBC. She passionately believes in the BBC's public service remit, and in showing women's sport. I have long theorised that she saw how Team GB's 2016 hockey gold lit up the nation and proved that there was audience interest in elite women's sport and that if you broadcast it, they will watch it. So it came as no surprise when she took the decision – regarded by some as bold and by others as a bit daft, and by me as brilliantly foresighted – to broadcast every game in the 2019 Women's World Cup live. Sure, some of the games were on the red button or on the digital channels, but when England reached the semi-final against the USA, with live coverage on BBC One, a true national moment was created. It attracted a peak audience of 11.7 million people, the most-watched TV event of the UK to that point in the year. The case was proven.

Back in my professional life, in 2018, an opportunity that seemed unmissable came up:

Women in Football – the leading organisation in the world to support women in the game – were looking for their first-ever CEO. Women in Football is an organisation with thousands of brilliant members. They are women and non-binary people, and men who support our aims. We are fans, we are players, we volunteer in the game and we work in the game. As an organisation, we exist to support, celebrate and champion our sisters in football and to drive positive change in the game and in the industry.

Have I experienced sexism working in football? Yes. Has it been harmful? Yes. Have I also encountered men who have been a great support to me? Yes, a lot of them. It is possible for women to work in football and thrive. Many have fulfilling, successful and rewarding careers. And yet our research at Women in Football tells us that 66 per cent of women working in football have experienced gender discrimination. What's more, the football industry is gendered. While there are tens of thousands of women who work across male professional football, they remain under-represented in senior roles and in pitch-side roles.

But football is an industry that's changing and that wants to be better. It needs a bit of a helping hand to make the change it wants, and that's where Women in Football comes in. We can help football to do better on diversity and to be more inclusive.

I did the job for three years and loved it. I saw a real change, as Women in Football's vision of a football industry where everyone can thrive and reach their full potential came ever closer to realisation. We've still a way to go, but we and the game are getting there. In late 2021 I decided to take my foot off the gas, and I stepped down as Women in Football CEO. I remain on the board, and I also do some work back in the male professional game with a focus on the academies, ensuring they comply with the detailed regime for the development of elite players that back in the day I had helped to draft.

As I sat on that bench near my home on the Saturday before the Euros final, I thought back through all of this, and my wonderful, 50-year roller coaster of a ride as a woman in football. I thought ahead to the following day and the final.

Soon football would be setting off on the next stage of its journey. I was beyond nervous, of course, but part of me was also thinking about how much this incredible game never fails to surprise me. Here we were, 30 years after I suggested that maybe one day the Lionesses could win the Euros, on the eve of seeing whether they could do exactly that.

2

THERE IS always an ulterior motive behind hosting a huge sporting competition. Governments love them because they build national soft power, make the nation feel good, and make the nation healthier if people are influenced to take up sport. Sports governing bodies love them because they make money and improve the profile of the sport.

There are additional considerations for women's sport. Our society does not prioritise seeing women's bodies as organisms created to walk, run, jump and kick. Rather, our sexual attractiveness is the primary lens through which our bodies are assessed. Elite women's sport disrupts this. It presents a new way of looking at women's bodies. It teaches all of us – women and men – that female bodies can and do exert speed, power and agility, and that these things should be practised and celebrated in their own right.

After centuries of being subject to the male gaze, this directly tackles women's internalised self-policing, that energy-sapping process whereby we constantly self-assess our bodies and find that they come up short against the unobtainable 'ideals' that are hammered into us. This is why playing football, for women, is about far more than kicking a ball. And it's why staging a huge women's football tournament has the power to change the world.

There was just a little bit at stake with these Euros, then. Talking to colleagues across the game in the run-up to the tournament, we all knew this. It wasn't just about the football, it was about the fight for respect and equality. This is a high burden for an England team playing at a home Euros to bear.

There was also the possibility of what a home Euros could do to grow the game in England. Finally taken seriously from around the turn of the millennium, and increasingly well led by The FA across this time, we had seen exciting increases in all metrics: participation, interest, revenue. Covid had paused our edition of the game in its tracks (and delayed these Euros by a year), and for a time in the spring of 2020 I was concerned that all the wonderful progress to that point would be lost. Happily, my fears were misplaced as women's football came roaring back after the pandemic, but if England did well in these Euros there was the opportunity for growth and expansion like nothing we had seen before this point.

Of course, my enjoyment of women's football tournaments is not just about changing the world. There's also the simple pleasure of watching the football as a fan, of living more or less in the moment and enjoying the licence to put aside workaday cares for 90 minutes of sporting excellence. But I'm an England fan, and I had a desire – tinged by desperation – for England to win. I didn't think they would. They were in the mix, but so were France, Germany, Spain, Norway, Sweden and the Netherlands. I wasn't sure this England team would come together and create something that was greater than the sum of its parts. But then, that may also be a reflection of the kind of football fan I am: namely one who is utterly convinced that everything will shortly end in disaster. It needs to be remembered that my father died from an appalling illness when I was 13: the root of my belief that everything is about to turn to absolute disaster is because when I was a girl, it did. Yet this doesn't stop me wanting success for my teams with all my heart, and somewhere having that tiny bit of hope that it may just happen. This is the agony of fandom, or at least my fandom: you want something so much, but you believe it highly unlikely to happen.

The tickets we had bought the previous summer were part of the record-breaking pre-tournament total ticket sales of 500,000. This didn't surprise me: the British public have a huge appetite for live sport, and not just football. Filling the London Olympic stadium for the 2012 Olympic Games was to be expected; filling it for the Paralympic Games was not – but it happened. Two million people had taken to the streets of Yorkshire to see the Grand Départ of the Tour de France two years later. Women's sport pulled them in too: 2019 saw the 11,000-capacity Liverpool Arena sell out for the Netball World Cup. But what was perhaps not quite business as usual was who had bought the tickets for these Euros: 43 per cent of them had been bought by women, and 21 per cent of total sales were children's tickets. Women and families would be attending the Euros in numbers.

All this was still to come when, on a Monday morning in late June 2022, a couple of weeks before the tournament started, I found myself in an empty corporate hospitality suite at the Gtech Community Stadium. The room looked out onto the silent stadium, resting in sunlight. There is nothing quite like an empty football stadium. The banks of empty seats have a poignancy – you can't help but think of the absent crowd. Above, there's always a trapezoid of sky bounded by the roofs of the stands. I have gazed at the trapezoid in an attempt to centre myself and control rising anxiety at countless matches in countless grounds. On this day at Brentford, the trapezoid showed a sky that was an empty, perfect blue. On the pitch, tall sprays of water from the sprinklers gently swayed first this way and then that way, thousands of tiny droplets catching the sun and falling softly onto immaculate grass. All around was the stillness of high summer and a sense of expectation. That moment was for me like opening a door in my football Advent calendar because I knew the pitch was being watered and pampered in preparation for hosting matches in the UEFA Women's Euros. The long wait was nearly over.

I was at Brentford that day to lecture on Women in Football's four-day Leadership Course. I adore teaching this course. I adore the women who attend it. At Women in Football, we all do. The course aims to help women working in football develop the skills they need to succeed as managers and leaders of the national game. It's a key component of delivering our vision of a football industry where everyone can thrive. It's also vital to football's future: if we want the football workforce in both the men's and women's game to be more diverse, we have to build the capacity of the talent pool. At Women in Football, we're proud to play our part in this and to work with the incredible women who come on our courses and listen, talk, share some of their profoundest concerns and thoughts, and go deep into themselves to understand who they are and how they can become better leaders.

At some point during that first day, someone wandered into the room, took in a group of women sat around a board table, and asked if it was the UEFA meeting about the Women's Euros that would be played here. I felt a little pull of excitement: suddenly the tournament was very real and present.

Two weeks later the Euros opened with England playing Austria in Manchester. In sharp contrast to the sunlit, pre-tournament peace of Brentford, Old Trafford had a hell-like quality as the teams walked out. The sound, the fury, the smoke from the fireworks obscuring the view of the pitch – there was something deep and a little dark about the tournament's opening minutes. The roar of the crowd in particular made us all catch our breath. The noise and atmosphere were incredible. 'Never thought I'd see the day,' I said on Twitter. Everyone was feeling it: 'emotional', 'magical', 'phenomenal' came the replies.

As the Lionesses walked out onto the pitch, some of them turned and applauded the crowd. Some of them stared straight ahead, unblinking. When the camera panned down their line as they sang 'God Save the Queen', we saw that captain Leah Williamson had her eyes tight shut as she sang. I worried that it was getting to her.

Sarina Wiegman, the England head coach who had already won the Women's Euros with the Netherlands, had tried several line-ups in the games in the year to date, but once the Euros kicked off she was never to vary her starting XI. Mary Earps was in goal, with Leah Williamson and Millie Bright at the heart of the defence, Lucy Bronze on the right, and Rachel Daly on the left. Keira Walsh and Georgia Stanway were in midfield, with Fran Kirby just in front of them. Lauren Hemp played wide on the left and Beth Mead on the right, with Ellen White up front. That opening night in Manchester, we hadn't seen this exact England line-up before.

The Lionesses gave us a positive but not earth-shattering performance, with a single goal from

Beth Mead enough to win it. I clocked some nice stuff – flashes of brilliant creativity from Fran Kirby, Millie Bright heading everything clear, Lucy Bronze's ability to spot several options where you think there's only one – but it hadn't quite gelled in front of goal, and this was a team we were expecting to score freely. All in all, England's performance was a little nervy, a little unsettled. Even Sarina Wiegman thought they could do better.

The real stars of the night were the 68,871 fans at Old Trafford, the largest-ever attendance in Women's Euros history (this record wasn't to last long, but we'll get to that). Engaged, passionate and noisy, they weren't afraid to show the world how good a time they were having. The players later said that the crowd was so loud they couldn't hear each other. When the record attendance was announced, the crowd roared. At the final whistle, they stayed behind and partied. And when you looked around, you saw more women and more children than at a Premier League game. A point had been proved: a women's football match can be both a family affair and a passionate, noisy spectacle.

I was glued to the TV as the rest of the runners and riders kicked off in the subsequent days. Spain, Germany and France each scored four or five goals in their first games. There you have it, I thought, that's how Euros winners start their campaigns, not with nervy 1-0s. The mental conflicts of my fandom kicked in: I'd never expected England to lead the pack, but I desperately *hoped* they would lead the pack. And here they were, most decidedly not leading the pack.

That was about to change.

But back in our non-football lives, we had to alter our summer plans. A combination of new work and personal circumstances meant that the following week was suddenly the only week of the summer when we'd be able to get ourselves away on a proper holiday. I love our football trips but, working in the game, they are not a full downing-of-the-tools and switching-off of the kind that I really need at least once a year. We could either use the coming week for a holiday like that or we'd have to forgo a proper break for the rest of the summer. So we took ourselves off to a caravan on the coast.

CHAPTER 2

The weather was gorgeous. We went into that deep laziness that is our usual holiday behaviour. Each day we'd sunbathe, read and sleep. In the late afternoon we'd stop lazing on sun loungers and start lazing on the caravan's sofas in front of the TV as the first of the day's two Euros games kicked off. We'd only move hours later at the final whistle of the second game.

Each day followed this glorious, dreamy, sun-filled, book-filled, football-filled pattern, and the day of the Lionesses' game against Norway was no exception. It was strange that, being such uber-fans, we were going to watch it on TV, but we've always been clear about the need for balance and proper rest in our leisure time. It was to turn out that watching this one on TV rather than at the Amex Stadium wasn't a bad option: there was going to be an awful lot to watch.

Ever the pessimist, I had confidently predicted that we would struggle against Norway's forward line, arguably the best in the world. Neither I nor anyone else had any inkling of what was about to happen.

The deluge started early. In the tenth minute, Ellen White got a soft penalty and Georgia Stanway converted it. Four minutes later Lauren Hemp made it 2-0. Then, 15 minutes later, Ellen White got her second.

The half-hour had only just passed and on England went. Beth Mead headed one home to make it 4-0. The first tentative chorus of 'Football's coming home' began to ring out around the Amex Stadium. A few minutes later Mead netted another. Not to be outdone, a couple of minutes later Ellen White scored her second, making it 6-0 to England.

Half-time and breeeeeeathe. There was bewildered excitement all around the Amex and all around the country. What had just happened? What were we watching here? We all struggled to process it, the BBC punditry team of Gabby Logan, Ian Wright, Alex Scott and Jonas Eidevall as ecstatic and slightly baffled as everyone else. We had just witnessed possibly the greatest half of football ever played by any England team.

In the second half, England made some substitutions, and for the first time we saw what power there was on the England bench. Ten minutes after replacing Ellen White, Alessia Russo made it 7-0. This time, there was nothing tentative about the way the crowd sang 'Football's coming home'. And just in case we were getting worried that we hadn't heard from Beth Mead in a while, with nine minutes to go she completed her hat-trick.

The final score was England 8, Norway 0 – the biggest win for any team, women or men, in any Euros ever. England had smashed their way into the quarter-finals, top of the group with a game in hand.

'What's going on?' said everyone afterwards, including Sarina Wiegman. The tweets came thick and fast: 'Sitting here in the stadium in disbelief.' 'Simply incredible.' 'Jesus Christ, wow, where do I start?' In their post-match interviews, Beth Mead and Ellen White shared the nation's elation and astonishment.

But I knew what I'd seen: an England team playing with speed, verve, style, skill, cohesion and aggression. And something else: they'd looked like they were enjoying themselves, and that they were enjoying playing with each other. They looked like they liked each other. I began to get a sense that there was a unity across this team.

Maybe if England had only beaten Norway 2-0, the country would not have woken up to what was going on like it did. There it is again: women have to work harder to prove themselves. Yes, there were questions about the Norwegian defence, but when Norway give you lemons, you've still got to make the lemonade. And England were flying, cruising, bossing it, playing creatively and confidently, playing in that way where you're barely conscious you're playing football at all because it feels like you're dancing.

The Dance of the Lionesses had begun.

* * *

In the days before the next game, I began what became an obsession with 'Lionesses Live', a programme streamed live on YouTube most days from the Lensbury Hotel in Teddington. After a long pre-tournament camp at St George's Park, The

FA's national training centre in Staffordshire, the team had moved to the Lensbury for the duration of the tournament. As a hotel, the Lensbury's fine, but what really sets it apart is that it has 25 acres of beautiful grounds that slope gently down to the River Thames. If, like the Lionesses, you have to be holed up with a couple of dozen other people for a few weeks, away from your loved ones and with limited ability to take a day for yourself, there are worse places to be.

A corner of the grounds was set up with decking, sofas, coffee tables and fairy lights, and from here Joelah Noble would broadcast 'Lionesses Live' most days. Joelah was usually joined by Abbie McCarthy, sometimes by other hosts. Both of them are young broadcasters and presenters, and I felt I wasn't quite the demographic that The FA were targeting. But I soon became hooked by the relaxed, jokey and fun tone. Much of this was set by Joelah and Abbie, but at the heart of the programme were the Lionesses themselves. One or two would come on to most of the programmes, and they'd open up to talk about the game they'd just played, or the goal they'd just scored, or life in the England camp with its trips to the coffee cart and competitiveness over the basketball machine. Then there was the fan interaction, with young girls brought in on Zoom or having their tweeted questions put to the Lioness of the day, sitting with Joelah and Abbie in the sun-soaked garden. The players were genuine, warm and grounded. And there it was again – that sense that not only were they at ease in themselves, but that they were at ease with each other.

England finished the group stage by playing Northern Ireland at Southampton. I have a professional interest in all the home nations teams, as Women in Football is a UK-wide organisation. Besides, narrow tribalism is not really my style. I'd followed much of the Northern Ireland story in the build-up to these Euros, and it had mostly caught my heart. I say 'mostly' because in April 2022 Kenny Shiels, the Northern Ireland manager, had said that girls and women concede second goals quickly because they 'are more emotional than men'. I thought back to the 'Born Kicking' days, when the headmaster of a local school told me that women had 'the wrong pelvic structure' for football (and I thought you needed a good right foot). Every aspect of our being can be and will be and has been picked on to explain why we are inadequate at football.

Shiels apologised for his comments, and we were able to move on and focus on the football. Northern Ireland were having their own fairy tale: they were playing in their first major tournament ever and the Irish FA, with full political support from across the country's fractured political spectrum, had put in place resources to allow the players to effectively be full-time for the months leading up to the final. And it was working: Valerie Heron, chair of the Northern Ireland Women's Football Association, told me, 'Everyone who doubted women's football in Northern Ireland has sat up and taken notice.'

Northern Ireland came to the England game having already been eliminated. In their earlier games, they'd been brave, they'd battled, they'd scored a goal to send the travelling Green and White Army wild. But they were playing the Lionesses for pride. And they managed to hold them for 40 proud minutes. Eventually, however, England romped home 5-0 winners.

The Northern Ireland players had made a difference, though. In October, the team were given a reception at Stormont. Kenny Shiels said they had brought the communities (note the plural) together. Player Joely Andrews talked charmingly of how, when they got off the plane at Southampton for the England game, 'the bus was waiting, we didn't even have to go into the building! … I felt like a superstar, it was so surreal!' Oh, Joely! May women's football never lose that wide-eyed wonder at a private jet.

This team, like all teams, were keen to inspire young girls, to show them that they too can play football. There was a plan for professionalisation of the Northern Irish women's league in 2023. Valerie Heron told me that the early signs after the tournament were that more youth teams and leagues were starting up. I wish them all the very best: their journey is our journey, their struggle our struggle. May many more Northern Irish players grace the pitch in elite competitions.

As for England, they had concluded their group stage by breaking another record: the highest number of goals scored by any team in the (men's or women's) Euros group stage. We had begun to see the strength that ran through this England team: the excellence in every position, the talent on the bench that could win us games late in the second half.

But we hadn't played the best teams yet.

* * *

The evening of the quarter-final against Spain, I was at a long-planned offsite meeting near Birmingham that simply had to take place on 20 July due to everyone's diaries. That day the British rail network quite literally melted in the heat. My train turned out to be about the only one that ran on the West Midlands main line. Going in the opposite direction was my Women in Football colleague Louise, a passionate and knowledgeable fan of women's football, whose journey to the quarter-final was horrendous. Thwarted by the melting rail network, she switched to a coach, which battled its way past motorway protestors to Gatwick Airport, where she picked up a train to Brighton. The journey took her eight hours.

I eventually got to the very pleasant hotel where the meeting would take place, but it was a hotel that had no public TV screens. I mean, there was a bar. Of course there was. But a TV in that bar? *Nada*.

Due to Covid, I hadn't met this group of people in the flesh for two long years. When we convened in the early evening for dinner, there was no question of me gulping something down quickly and rushing back to my room. These are good people, and we work well together, and I wanted to spend time with them. So we propped up my phone in the middle of the table, and every five minutes or so, one of us would bend down to have a look, and from time to time I would flick the sound up.

I did not at all like what I was seeing and hearing. Every time the sound went up, the BBC commentator was talking in anxious tones about the Spanish attack, the Spanish tide, rising Spanish confidence, the Spanish mastery of the ball. It was agony. At some point late in the second half, I did one of my checks of the screen and my heart hit the floor. Spain were leading 1-0. *Oh no*, I thought, *oh no*. Conversation round the table had been flowing. A combination of not wanting to let what looked like England's likely exit from the Euros spoil dinner and of wanting to distract myself from the emotional load that defeat would bring, meant that I decided to turn the phone off.

I didn't find out that England had won until I was walking back to my room after dinner. In the hotel corridor, I flicked the phone on. When I saw the score, my hand went up to my mouth, tears came to my eyes, and I muttered 'Oh my god, oh my god.'

In my room, I sat up pressing refresh on BBC iPlayer until the match in its entirety appeared online at some point after midnight. I watched the whole damn thing, there and then. What I saw was Spain playing their tiki-taka possession style of play *par excellence*. Their plan was to wear England down by keeping possession and keeping England in their own half. It nearly worked. During the first half, while England weren't without moments, Spain were constantly attacking, relentlessly hungry for the ball, incessantly playing fast, neat passes at the highest tempo. It looked exhausting to defend against – physically and mentally. But here's the thing: England didn't tire. They kept working it, defending it, attacking when they could.

It was hell to watch, even though I knew the score. But two things came together to turn it round. The first was that the crowd never, ever stopped. Lucy Bronze later said that they made all the difference. The second was that Sarina Wiegman had a Plan B.

Plan B involved England moving to having three, not four, in defence. This released Millie Bright – our central defender of the messy blonde topknot, who boots and heads everything (well, nearly everything) clear – to go up front. This was exciting. It had the potential to shake things up, to unsettle the Spanish defence. And if you want to talk about possession football, let's talk about a movement that started with the goalkeeper and was worked down the pitch by eight different players without the opposition getting a foot on it. Only it wasn't Spain who did this, it was England. The last of the eight English players to touch the ball was Ella Toone, and it went into the net.

1-1. The 84th minute and it was 1-1.

All hell broke loose. The Amex erupted in noise, relief and ecstasy. On the touchline Sarina – cool, calm Sarina – started dancing. The Spanish players hectored and challenged the referee. The Spanish bench hectored and challenged the fourth official. Bizarrely, the Spanish third-choice keeper was such a pain in the neck in this mêlée off the pitch that she got booked.

Neither team could wrap things up in normal time and so an extra half-hour was played. In the end, England settled it early on in the extra period with a wonderful goal from Georgia Stanway to make it 2-1 and send England through to the semi-finals. Even to this day, watching this goal on replay for the 20th time, I cry.

So England got the win, but this was the game that nearly burst the bubble. England had been six minutes away from leaving their home Euros. They had faced their toughest test yet – one of their toughest tests ever – and they had come through. The fact that Millie Bright, a central defender, was player of the match says all you need to know about how under pressure England had been. But there was also a sense that England had unprecedented belief, determination and resilience, with every Englishwoman on the pitch doing her job to the utmost of her ability for the full length of the game, and playing for every other team-mate. Nevertheless, I couldn't help but feel that England were fundamentally beatable. For some, such as my colleague Louise, the victory was the moment when the belief that England could win became absolutely cemented. But I'm not that kind of fan, and I still didn't have them marked down as potential tournament winners.

There was a depressing post-script for this Spanish team: a month or so after the tournament finished, 15 players confronted the Spanish Federation and asked for changes to the national team's working conditions, with concerns reportedly centring around training, preparation and coaching, perhaps in contrast to the high standards of all these things that they experienced at their clubs. They were absent from the team sheets for Spain's first games after the Euros, the Federation claiming they'd 'resigned', and the players claiming the Federation had barred them from selection until they apologised. This was women footballers struggling for something better, making their voices heard, but without the mechanisms for their concerns to be acted on.

The optics were, frankly, dreadful as the Spanish Federation high-ups were all men, and it looked like men ignoring and crushing women's voices. Spain are a team who grace the women's game. The job of the Spanish Federation is to make sure their strongest players are at the 2023 World Cup. Elite football has to put players front and centre of everything and to make room for the difficult conversations. As we will see, it has often failed to do so, with devastating results.

* * *

England travelled to Sheffield and Bramall Lane for the semi-final against Sweden. My inner doomsayer continued its work after the quarter-final, and I counselled anyone who'd listen that Sweden, the Olympic Games silver medallists, were ranked second in the world and there was considerable doubt over how England would fare.

What there was no doubt about was the Swedish fans. With Sweden having played two of their group-stage games at Sheffield, they'd taken a bit of ownership of the city. On the warm but overcast afternoon before the semi-final, they banged their drums and sang their songs outside the Frog & Parrot, and then a sea of yellow shirts and blue-and-yellow wigs and bucket hats marched to Bramall Lane, drumming and chanting.

England nearly went a goal down after only 20 seconds. 'See you at Wembley,' read one of the Swedish banners in the stands. As the Swedish drums that had marched from the Frog & Parrot rumbled away in the stands, it didn't look like an over-optimistic statement. But about halfway through the first half, England began to find a little more rhythm, and just after the half-hour Mead belted home a Lucy Bronze cross. 1-0 to England.

When your team go 1-0 up just after the half-hour, obviously you're pleased, but often your thoughts run along the lines of '*Great, let's get to half-time, and then let's hang on to this score in the second half.*' Yet, even with my cautious view, I'd begun to sense that this free-scoring Lionesses team had now found its path to goal and that there could well be more to come.

So it proved. Lucy Bronze headed in a corner. Our initial delight was quickly muted as there was a VAR check, but then Bramall Lane erupted. Then, just short of the hour, Sarina Wiegman made one of her usual substitutions: Alessia Russo came on for Ellen White to give England fresh power up front. And it worked. Oh my god, it worked.

Now, imagine it's a European Championship semi-final, and you're Alessia Russo, and the ball lands at your feet right in front of goal. You strike but straight at the keeper. You should have done better and you know it. The ball bounces off the keeper, though, and you get in a tussle for it with a Swedish defender. There the pair of you are, side by side, battling for the ball, backs to the goal. And suddenly, somehow, you backheel the ball. You *backheel* it. And you don't just backheel it – *you nutmeg the keeper*. You weren't even looking but you backheel it through the keeper's legs and into the goal.

Whether we were at Bramall Lane or in a fan park or in a living room, we were all jumping and screaming and wide-eyed in wonder all at once. What on earth had we just seen? On the screen, Russo ran triumphantly, fists clenched tight and arms aloft and ramrod-straight like two knitting needles stuck in a ball of wool. It was absolutely the best, the craziest, the cheekiest, the most glorious goal I have ever seen.

And this was the moment. This was the moment when even the terminally anxious like me didn't just dare to dream but began to allow ourselves a smidgeon of belief: we were going to Wembley.

Afterwards, having adored the goal, I adored how Russo talked about it. She expressed annoyance she hadn't scored the first chance, and that what she did after that miss just seemed to her the quickest route back to goal. She wasn't grandiose, she wasn't boastful (though she had every right to be). She was real and relatable. While she and all the Lionesses had of course benefited from extensive media training, it was more evidence of a rounded, grounded team.

But that came later. Because England hadn't finished with Sweden. In the 77th minute Fran Kirby, who'd had a wonderful game, chipped the ball just outside the 18-yard box. Time stood still as she and all of us froze and watched the flight of the ball. The keeper leapt, got two hands to it and pushed it up. We all watched the ball's ascent and descent – and into the net it went.

An absolute party began. No one could doubt this now. We were going to Wembley. When the final whistle went, Ellen White was in tears. Beth Mead and Jill Scott beamed with delight. Mary Earps leapt into Millie Bright's arms. Sarina Wiegman hugged everyone, including all the technical staff. The players got into their post-match circular huddle. We couldn't see what Sarina was saying to them, but we could see a ring of bright smiles.

The huddle broke up and the team danced over to the fans as the DJ put 'Sweet Caroline' on. 'How much fun is this?' asked BBC Radio 5 Live. Good times really never had seemed so good. Bramall Lane was rocking, with everyone jumping in the stands, everyone singing. 'I look round, it's not just women, it not just young girls. It's men, it's young boys,' said Stephen Warnock on the radio. I thought back to Lucy Bronze speaking at a Women in Football members' event in 2020 when said she wanted to be a role model not just to young girls but to young boys as well.

The camera focused on eight-year-old Tess Dolan, whose free and joyous dancing in the stands to 'Sweet Caroline' immediately elevated her to national poster girl and cheerleader-in-chief. 'We call her our sunshine,' her mum said later. In that moment, she was the nation's sunshine, capturing how we all felt. She stood as an avatar for every girl, every woman jumping, dancing and air-punching for the joy of football.

On BBC One, the commentary team were in the same mix of ecstasy and shock as the rest of us. But Ian Wright got serious, and addressed the nation: 'If girls are not now allowed to play football in their PE lessons just like the boys are, then what are we doing?' What indeed? Back on Radio 5, Everton player and former Lioness Izzy Christiansen was asked what could stop this England team.

'Nothing,' she said. 'You can't stop them.'

3

WHAT DO you do the day after winning the semi-final of the UEFA European Championship? If you're the Lionesses, there's a fixed post-match routine that doesn't change just because the next game is the final. Indeed, keeping to the same routines and the same processes means everything and everyone stays grounded as you head back from Sheffield to the Lensbury and the seclusion of its lawns sloping down to the Thames. If you played, you do cryotherapy (you get to sit in a freezer for a couple of minutes). If you didn't, you train. You have your dinner. The next day you have a day off – maybe a boat trip down the Thames, maybe some music, maybe a stroll to the coffee shop – all very chilled.

Time and again when the Lionesses were interviewed, they spoke of how Sarina Wiegman was level-headed and had unchanging processes in place throughout the tournament. 'She's very logical, she doesn't allow us to overthink, she keeps everyone focused on the task,' said Jill Scott two days before the final. Keira Walsh talked of how relaxed the group was, and of how Sarina 'gives everyone confidence, that's the main thing. That is the base of everything we do. Everyone feels confident and everyone feels valued.'

In the four days before the final, the Lionesses kept it calm, kept it normal, and worked hard. You could even watch a YouTube livestream of their final day's training and see the strength, the intent, the focus, the sheer hard work of these women. In the weeks and months to come they'd do fashion shoots and lifestyle pieces and reality shows. But the foundation of all this, and the essence of what they are, is their approach to their sport: dedicated, hard-working, focused. Watching the live training, there wasn't a slacker among them.

Elsewhere, however, we were all going a little crazy. Everyone was joining the party. The messages of support and congratulations came flooding in from Jordan Henderson, Declan Rice, Wayne Rooney, David Beckham, Lewis Hamilton, and little Princess Charlotte sitting on her dad's knee in a cute Twitter video. The nation was smiling. Sure, the flag of St George didn't appear in as many windows as it would do for the men (although respect to the Kirby Estate of London SE16, who properly went for it with the flags, then felt that wasn't enough and so unveiled a giant mural of their namesake Fran). But the national delight was genuine and deep, and I cannot regret the fact that it lacked some of the angst, urgency, expectation and pressure that comes with supporting the men's team.

The day after England's victory against Sweden we watched Germany beat France in the second semi-final. The scene was set. It would be England v Germany at Wembley on 31 July. The global women's football establishment began to descend on London. On the Monday of that week, one of my colleagues in the men's game asked if I was up to much before the final. 'Oh yeah, there's a load of conferences and drinks parties and that,' I replied. He opened his eyes and pursed his lips in gentle mocking. 'Ooh, get you,' he said. It was a fair comment, and I laughed. I felt a little like Northern Ireland's Joely Andrews and her wide-eyed wonder at the team's private plane.

At the various events in that week before the final, it felt like the family had come together. One of the main events was a conference organised by the NGO Equal Playing Field. I spoke on one of the conference's panels about whether we should care who owns our football clubs (short answer: we should), but for me the real pleasure was listening to the fantastic talks on a host of topics about the women's game: how to grow it, where that growth should focus, male allyship, player activism, fan culture in the women's game, and many others.

The most powerful talk of the two days came from Khalida Popal, the guiding light of women's football in Afghanistan, where it briefly flourished before the Taliban re-established their woman-hating tyranny. When the Taliban took power, women footballers (many of whom were too young to remember much about the Taliban's previous regime) had to flee for their lives. But even when women could play in Afghanistan, they couldn't do so without encountering the unique type of evil that some men reserve for women: members of the women's national team were sexually abused by men in the Afghanistan Football Federation. 'That system of football's brotherhood, the gatekeepers, allowed so many of my women to be raped and abused,' said Khalida.

Allegations of sexual abuse of female footballers have also surfaced in many other countries – the Netherlands, Venezuela, Canada and the USA, for starters. Earlier in July, former Dutch national team player Vera Pauw revealed that during her playing career, she had been raped by a Dutch football official and sexually assaulted by two other men. She criticised the Dutch FA, saying 'some people would rather keep my rape and sexual assaults quiet than offer support'. In 2019, former Vancouver Whitecaps player Ciara McCormack

CHAPTER 3

blew the whistle on inappropriate behaviour and
abuse by a senior coach in the Canadian women's
game 11 years previously. That's quite a time gap,
but it wasn't the first time she'd told her story – and
nothing had truly been done to address it in those
11 years.

Worse was to come in the autumn, but at that
point, having been reminded at the conference of
the harm that is inflicted on women, and indeed
having been slightly retraumatised (for I have my
own story about something that happened to me
as a teenager – not in football, but enough to lay
down deep scars), I trotted off to the light-hearted
fripperies of the drinks parties with gratitude. It was
time to simply be a football fan for a couple of days.

When I woke up on Saturday 30 July, there
was an empty day in front of me, which meant
there was nothing going on to fill my head. Which
meant I would fill it myself – and I duly proceeded
to cram it full of the weight of history and worry
about the match the next day. I cast about on
Twitter a bit to find what other people were doing.
Yvonne Harrison, the Women in Football CEO,

was preparing to watch the football on Sunday by watching some more football (Man City v Liverpool in the Community Shield) on this Saturday. At Knowle Ladies and Girls FC, one of the stalwarts of female grassroots football in the West Midlands, they were washing and folding and refolding the training bibs slightly obsessively. Ali Speechly, an experienced and fantastic coach, suggested focusing on the moment and not thinking too much about the end, which was brilliant advice, and I managed it for about half an hour. But in the end I had to take myself to the bench by the railway line on the way to the supermarket.

It felt surreal that the day of the final should also be the start of the men's English Football League season, and it was happenstance that the opening televised fixture on that day was Sunderland v Coventry. It kicked off at 12 noon, which would give us more than enough time to watch it and then after its final whistle to get to Wembley for the start of the Euros final at 5pm.

My friend Helen supports Sunderland. Her husband, Ben, supports Coventry. They live a few miles from us, all of us incomers to the south-east in our youth. Ben and Helen had tickets for the final, so we agreed that they would come to our house, Ben would put up with watching Sunderland v Coventry in the company of three Sunderland fans, and then we'd all set off for Wembley together. When I opened the front door to them, they stood on the threshold looking both giggly and guilty. Helen was carrying a couple of carrier bags and she looked at me intently, as if judging what kind of mood I was in. One of the carrier bags was thrust at me. It had the expected offering of booze, to go with the food I'd prepared. She hung on to the other plastic bag. The giggling and the furtive looks continued.

We sat, drinks were poured, the food I'd prepared was picked at, and then Helen, still clutching the second plastic bag, said, 'You know that thing you said?'

'It isn't …' I replied.

'It is!' and she thrust the carrier bag at me.

Rewind a year to the summer of 2021, and us buying our tickets. I came out then with a bold statement that I was to repeat over the following months, and several times during the course of the Euros: 'If we get to the final, I'm wearing a Millie Bright wig.'

Why Millie Bright? Most of the Lionesses' team had long hair, most of them blonde (and usually with two inches of dark root because you can't get to your colourist when you're on an England camp). Most of them pulled their hair back tightly, and England goal celebrations were often a throng of flying blonde ponytails. Millie Bright had a different solution: her blonde hair all got bundled up on top into a huge knot, inevitably with quite a few stray, messy, wispy bits. There was something a little blowsy about the result, and I absolutely loved it. Out from the plastic bag came the most realistic recreation of it I have ever seen. We all tried it on, took ridiculous photos, cried laughing.

I barely followed the Sunderland game. All the stuff from the previous day on the bench was buzzing round and round in my head again and, even though this was Sunderland's first game back in the Championship after four years, it seemed like

I was floating above the room, looking down on it, not really part of it. I watched in detached fashion as Sunderland scored early and Coventry equalised late. *Oh well*, I thought at the final whistle, *oh well*. My phone buzzed to say that our taxi had arrived. It was time to go.

This had been a bright, burning summer so far, and Sunday 31 July was no exception, with the temperature in the high twenties – most definitely T-shirt (mine saying 'I Am The Twelfth Woman') and shorts weather for Wembley. And then there was our England flag. We'd bought it in 2011 to take to the Women's World Cup in Germany, and one warm evening in Wolfsburg I'd spent far more hours than I'd planned drawing and colouring in a letter in each quadrant: S A F C. Club and country. Sunderland and England.

I confess, most times when I go to football these days, it's in the kind of seats where bringing your England flag with your club's initials badly drawn on in felt pen would be a little frowned upon. And I don't think I've ever seen anyone in the posh seats wearing a player-tribute wig. But today we were going just as fans. We arrived at Wembley a couple of hours before kick-off and so, with no prawn-sandwich platters to head for, there was plenty of time to walk round the stadium and take in the day.

I had started coming to Wembley regularly as soon as I moved to London in the late 1980s. Back then, of course, it was the 'old' Wembley, with its twin towers and the atrocious views from where they'd put seats in the old standing areas. The surrounding area, or the bit of it you saw as a football fan, was terrible. Unless you were going to football, there was no reason to visit Wembley, and the grand old stadium itself was surrounded by scruffy warehouses and car parks.

The 'grand old stadium', did I say? In many ways, it was a stadium of its times and not particularly comfortable. People may scoff but I like to be able to see the match, buy food and drink, and go to a clean toilet – none of which was guaranteed. But those twin towers were something else. Utterly iconic. Their demolition 20 years ago was controversial and, while I love the new arch that's replaced them, to me it hasn't quite become the visible symbol of the home of English football that the twin towers were. In one very important respect, though, the new Wembley stands shoulder to shoulder with the old Wembley: it is, as its predecessor was, the supreme cathedral of the English game. Every fan of every team wants to get there, and no matter how many times your team gets there, every trip is special. There is no more important destination in the game. Personally, I have never emerged from Wembley Park tube station and stood at the top of the stairs that lead down to Wembley Way, taking in the view of the stadium, without being moved. And I've taken in that view while on my way to many meetings at The FA, not just on my way to games. It gets me every time.

What to do when you arrive at a cathedral two hours before the main event? You wander around, you look at your fellow pilgrims, you drink in the atmosphere. We made our way to the stadium steps and looked back down Wembley Way. Even two hours before kick-off, it seemed full of thousands of people, happily milling around in the sunshine – women, men, children. So many children, so many women. So many white England shirts. Grown men and little girls with the cross of St George painted on their faces. Women wearing their England flags like cloaks, as I was. There was a low buzz of chatter, and the odd hooter blasting out a distinctive rhythm and getting the shouted reply 'England!' from a few voices.

Just as the stadium has been reborn, so has much of the suburb of Wembley. There are all the bells and whistles of 21st-century urban regeneration – snazzy office and apartment blocks, retail centres, gleaming bars and restaurants – but there's some fantastic public provision too: a new town hall with a brand-new library, and soon there will be one of London's newest parks on the site of a former stadium car park.

Looking back on that day, it's tempting to weave a narrative of transformation – for the national stadium as well as for the town around it. For the national game too, with the women about to play in front of nearly 90,000 people.

And while that narrative would be true, let's go back in time 12 months: if you'd been standing on Wembley Way on 11 July 2021, you'd have seen quite another scene. That was the day of another Euros final, also involving England – but this time it was the men. And it was very, very different. According to the Baroness Louise Casey's independent review of what happened, on that day Wembley Way and our stadium-cathedral witnessed an orgy of 'drunkenness, drug taking, irresponsibility, criminality, and abuse of innocent people', nearly resulting in 'fatalities and/or life-changing injuries for some, potentially many, in attendance'.

Take that in: only one year previously, people had nearly died at a football final at this place. I'd avoided that match: it's taken me a long time to get over going to England v Norway (men) at the Old Wembley in 1992, when the bloke behind me said for the entire game (including half-time): 'F*ck off, you f*cking Norwegians. Norwegians, f*ck off.' After nearly two hours of this droning, hate-filled monotone, my head was battered, and I came away promising myself never again to bother with England men's games at Wembley.

I've been to a few England men's games since then, but I really wasn't fussed about this one. And just as well. I started hearing from people there about what was going on before kick-off, and their reports continued over the next couple of days. The experience of one of my friends wasn't untypical: she was caught up when an entrance for disabled spectators was charged and she was nearly knocked to the ground. Later, she had to endure inappropriate bodily contact on Wembley Way. She called me a few days after the game and said, 'Jane, I think I'm having PTSD.'

There was widespread drug use and 6,000 ticketless fans, around 2,000 of whom managed to get into the stadium. Baroness Casey's review found failures in planning and control by those tasked with the safety of spectators and, while calling for those to be addressed without fail, it did not hesitate to lay the principal blame on 'the behaviour of a large minority of England supporters [which] was not just disgraceful, it recklessly endangered lives.'

I still find it hard to get across how shocking I find it that in 2021, more than 30 years after the Hillsborough disaster, a major football match endangered lives. I was a young woman and a football fan who regularly went to games when Hillsborough happened. At the time, I didn't know that I would go on to have a career in football, but it's fair to say that once I had started working in the game it was always there in the back of my mind. Having worked extensively in football governance, I am sometimes asked what the main duties of football club directors are. I am absolutely clear about the first and most important duty: make sure everyone goes home safely. Do this if you do nothing else.

Fast-forward to 2022 and another England team are about to play at another UEFA Euros final – and it's an utterly different world. What's the difference? Gender. We can't ignore it. Women's football crowds tend not to get off their heads on cocaine and charge disabled entrances. I should say in fairness that this kind of behaviour tends to attach itself to the men's national team; crowds for male club games at Wembley are nowhere near as anti-social and criminal, and they too are overwhelmingly male. And of course it's not all fans. Nevertheless, we sometimes talk a lot about what women's football can learn from men's football, but there's a lot that the men's game can learn from the women's. How to create a happy, hate-free crowd is one such thing. Merle Frohms, the German goalkeeper, said later: 'Even when we arrived on the bus, they were all waiting and applauding us. That's what differentiates women's football a bit: they were English fans but you could feel that they were happy to have us there and they were looking forward to the game.'

We were indeed. Our little group of four walked round the entire perimeter of Wembley, then took selfies in front of the Bobby Moore statue before heading inside. We bought drinks and food with ease and sat at tables where there was plenty of space and light flooding in through the windows. I adjusted my Millie Bright wig and stuck a Euros flag in its top-knot.

The SAFC on our flag got us the attention of the Ritson family from Sunderland: dad Paul, and daughters Annabel, who coached a girls' Under-14 side in the North-East, and 13-year-old Alice, who played for Sunderland AFC. Like us, they were having something to eat and drink before they took their seats and they were all nervous, all taking things in. This was far from their first trip to watch the Lionesses, and far from their first trip to Wembley, but the girls in particular were drinking in the experience of being here on this day, for this game.

Before long, it was time. At 4.45pm, 15 minutes before kick-off, we took our seats. As soon as I did so, I was overwhelmed. Jesus Christ almighty. The seats were near full, the noise was intense, the pitch was shining green. English and German flags were flying. The entire spectacle, the realisation that we were here for this, that women's football was doing it, that the Lionesses were doing it, that it was game on, that something I'd mentioned 30 years ago might happen was actually happening ... Jesus Christ almighty indeed. I caught my breath – literally. As an asthmatic I have to be sensitive to my lungs tightening up, and I felt them give a little 'oh hello'.

Annabel Ritson told me later she cried on taking her seat. The family were sitting just underneath the BBC's presentation team, and when Annabel looked up she could see Ian Wright taking photos, as though he was trying to take in the unprecedented moment and atmosphere as much as any of us.

There were over 87,000 people in Wembley, the largest attendance for any match in any European Championship (men's or women's) ever. The enormity of the occasion was almost unbearable. And yet the catch in my chest wasn't just because of this. It was also because Wembley was steamy. So hot, so humid. Wembley is one big continuous bowl with no natural air flow through it, and we were going to be sat there for at least two hours. I stared up at the sky. We were at the west end of Wembley, and I looked over at the other end. The clouds had dispersed and there was a trapezoid of bright sunlight falling on a huge section of the crowd. *The poor buggers must be roasting*, I thought.

Through all the hoopla that happened before the teams come out – the singer, the fireworks, the mini-blimps floating above the pitch with muslin banners falling from them – I focused on relaxation and breathing. But that was thrown aside when the teams came out, a moment that I want to hold for ever. Twenty-two proud, beautiful women strode into the cauldron and were greeted by a Wembley roar as loud as any roar I have ever heard at any football match anywhere. Whatever was to come next, here was history being made before our eyes.

The four of us stood and watched as the teams lined up. The German national anthem was played. This may be an unfashionable opinion, but I think it a glorious piece of Haydn and it was deeply moving to see this wonderful German team and their coach Martina Voss-Tecklenburg – a woman I respect so much – sing it with focus and pride. They are our sisters and we are united in our fight. Then a drumroll, and Wembley roared out 'God Save the Queen'. At Old Trafford, captain Leah Williamson had kept her eyes tight shut during the national anthem. This time they were open, and there was a smile on her face as she sang.

The teams were read out. At Millie Bright's name I jumped up and down, screaming '*Millie!*' and raising and lowering the wig, much to the amusement of two Scottish guys behind us. My friend Helen later asked them if they were doing that Scottish thing and supporting Germany against England, and they replied that if it was a men's match they most definitely would be, but that women's football was different and they liked this Lionesses team. Dear old football, sometimes it breaks down barriers rather than reinforces them.

The captains exchanged pennants. The tiny car brought the ball to the centre circle. The knee was taken. An all-female RAF crew led a fly-past of a Hercules and two Typhoon jets over Wembley. I was nearly overcome at the sight of bold, bright, brilliant women on the pitch, and bold, bright, brilliant women in the skies. Later, I tweeted Mandy Hickson, former RAF Tornado pilot, to say how wonderful it was to see our two worlds come together – #WomeninFootball and #WomeninJets. She replied that she could not have been prouder. Recollecting the fly-past continues to move me very deeply because, at that moment, the whole of creation – the earth and the sky – felt like it belonged to powerful women.

And so to kick-off. When you watch a match like this with so much at stake for something you care so profoundly about, you can end up in a mildly dissociative state. In the broiling heat of Wembley, everything seemed real, unreal and surreal at the same time. This strange, connected-but-disconnected feeling was emphasised when we learned that, despite early announcements that both sides were unchanged from the semi-finals, Germany's talismanic striker, Alexandra Popp, had not started. She'd scored in every game so far and was level with Beth Mead on six goals: among other things, this final was a race to see which of them would win the golden boot. It was only the next day that I heard she'd pulled up in the warm-up and was unable to start. I'm sorry she missed this showcase game; it should have been the pinnacle of her career.

But by then the match was under way. It started as it was to continue for two long hours of play: full-on, hard-fought, open, attacking football. Neither side was tentative. Neither side relented. On and on both teams attacked and tackled and passed and ran and fouled and pressed and defended. The first half was end to end, both sides playing with all they had. Both came close but matched each other, and neither was able to bring just that little edge of flair or genius that could have broken through.

It was torture. I desperately, hopelessly scrabbled for some kind of control in a situation that was so clearly beyond my control. There was nothing I could do, but that didn't stop my mind reaching for reasons and solutions. *The referee's not up to it and shouldn't have booked Stanway and White*, I reasoned. *Although White shouldn't have given the ref that bit of chatter and then she wouldn't have booked her*, I continued. *When oh when will this end*, I mentally nattered on to myself.

Half-time came. I looked with relief at the time on the big screen. Win or lose, there was only an hour to go, and then this agony would be over. Helen and Ben were likewise feeling an overwhelming sense of tension. My partner was a little calmer. He was one of the people – and I met a few on this journey – who had faith that England would win. Having watched the Lionesses for over a decade, he thought they finally had a manager who could change things around if the team found themselves in difficulty.

Things were to get worse before they got better. At the start of the second half, Germany made a change and substitute Tabea Wassmuth brought new energy and attack to Germany. From our position high in the stands, it looked like England were on the point of collapse. I felt ill. Helen put her hand on my shoulder in support.

But Sarina Wiegman always has a plan. Ella Toone and Alessia Russo came on, and about five minutes later Keira Walsh played one of the greatest balls ever from deep in the England half to behind the German defence. Ella Toone ran. We roared. Toone kept running. We kept roaring. Toone got the ball and chipped it over the German keeper into the goal.

I screamed. Helen screamed. Ben screamed. My partner screamed. Everyone around us screamed. In the posh seats, Prince William stood up and clapped (and, for all I know, maybe he screamed too). Wembley lit up as tens of thousands of women, men and children found their collective voice. I've heard Wembley roar many times. Just a couple of months earlier, the hairs had stood up on the back of my neck as half of Wembley roared out Sunderland's anthem 'Can't Help Falling in Love With You'. But here I was struck by the higher pitch of this roar. I don't think I've ever been somewhere where there were so many women shouting.

There was to be no shutting up of shop by England, no parking the bus. Instead, the game fell back into its pattern of attacking and pressing by both teams, with action in both boxes. Somehow, being 1-0 up with 25 minutes to go is a different kind of agony from 0-0, and the spell following England's goal was torture. I just didn't think England would hang on.

And then: *no, no, no, oh God help me, no.* Germany scored. It was a goal of similar quality to England's. It had a beautiful pass and great control and wonderful touches and a stunning volley. You had to admire it. You had to feel crushed that it had been scored.

Around me everyone was silent and frozen. We were back to square one. Surely we were going to extra time? So it proved and at the final whistle, my thoughts were all about self-management through the next 30 minutes. I felt trapped, a prisoner of football. *Why oh why do I do this?* I asked myself for about the 40th time that day. I looked up to the trapezoid, reminding myself that there was a world beyond this.

The teams battled through the first 15 minutes of extra time. It remained as tough and full-on as it had been all game. Just before the end of the first period, substitute Jill Scott was first caught by the German defender and then caught on camera using industrial language.

When the first period ended, I was somehow sure it wouldn't go to penalties. I didn't know who would win – both teams were tiring, and I couldn't see a way through for either of them – but I knew it wasn't going to penalties. Penalties are no way to end a journey that's taken a hundred years, and

I just felt certain that the football deities wouldn't allow it.

Shortly after the restart, Chloe Kelly won a corner and turned to the crowd. With both arms she signalled to us to raise the volume. Tens of thousands of us responded, because we are the Twelfth Woman. I stood up and, perhaps inspired by Jill Scott letting her voice be heard, I shouted and shouted, louder than I've ever shouted – uninhibited, not caring who was watching, not caring that women aren't supposed to shout. This was the European Championship Final and I was going to shout my damn head off.

And then it happened. Lauren Hemp took the corner. Lots of heads went up for the ball and it fell at Chloe Kelly's feet. She stabbed at it wildly and missed. But somehow it fell to her again, and this time there was no mistake.

Stop all the clocks.

England, oh England.

2-1.

I felt like I was taking off and floating up to the sky. I remembered how I'd felt myself falling when

Ian Porterfield had scored for Sunderland in the 1973 FA Cup Final. Two Wembley goals to bookend my 50 years as a woman in football: one scored by a man, which made me fall, and one scored by a woman, which made me fly.

For a couple of seconds Chloe Kelly sprinted away as Wembley screamed its heart out. Then there was a pause – was this going to a VAR check? No! And Chloe did something that has mythic status in women's sport: she took her shirt off. She ran ecstatically round the pitch in her sports bra. Chloe was not parading herself in her bra for male approval. This was a woman presenting her superb, strong, skilful body on her own terms as a thing of glory. It's an image that will be famous for ever.

Some people thought back to the American player Brandi Chastain, who had taken her shirt off after scoring the winning goal in the 1999 World Cup Final. But I wasn't sure this was what had inspired Chloe Kelly, as at that time she would only have been a year old. I was delighted to learn later from Beth Mead's autobiography that Chloe may have been channelling Bobby Zamora, who'd scored the winner in the last minute of the 2014 Championship play-off final for her beloved Queens Park Rangers. Like me, Chloe's football is grounded in being a fan of one of England's less fashionable football teams.

I thought back to Hostile Question Number Two that I would get asked in the 1990s: do you all swap shirts at the end? Well, you know what, sometimes we do, fella. And when we do, it isn't for your benefit, it's for ours. It's to celebrate our power and our joy. And yet, what I find moving about the image of Kelly isn't the sports bra. No, it's the bright-green grass stains on her white shorts and socks. They tell a story of graft and of a battle hard-fought and hard-won. None of this is easy. For elite players, football dominates their young lives. The team on the pitch had toiled for so long and given up so much for this moment. And there were others in the years before them, the people who'd laid the foundations on which this team was built. To fight against the 1921 ban, to bring our game here where, at long last, a capacity crowd could roar for a young woman putting her country at the top of Europe – it was a century's work.

The minutes ticked away slowly. In front of me, a young boy turned round to look at us because he couldn't watch the match, tension writ large across his face. I tried to smile at him, but what came out was a rictus of anguish.

England took the ball to the corner and kept it there – game management or poor sportsmanship? Weirdly, in the agony of the closing minutes, I remember being mildly annoyed at it. *Play up and play the game! Win with glory!* But my emotions were all over the place and I still thought Germany would sneak it. In the League One play-off final earlier in the season, I'd begun to have a sneaking suspicion with 20 minutes to go that Sunderland might actually win. Here, there was also a moment when I thought, *Oh my god, maybe we're going to win.* It came with 15 seconds to go.

When the final whistle blew, my partner stood in shock, not at first believing that England had finally won a major championship. I sat down and waited for the overwhelming emotions that I'd rehearsed on the bench the previous day. And then I thought, *Ah, don't be so ridiculous*, and stood up.

'Three Lions' was playing, and Wembley roared it out. I roared it out too, and so did my partner and Helen and Ben as we jumped and danced and waved the England flag with the felt-tip SAFC in the corners.

One hundred years of hurt had never stopped us dreaming.

Women's football was back where it belonged. It was home.

4

WOMEN'S FOOTBALL was home, and it was given a proper welcome. The party began on the final whistle. The Lionesses sang and danced, and ran away from media interviews to join in the giant karaoke of 'Sweet Caroline'. They lay on the pitch and made snow angels in the fallen glitter-confetti that had exploded into the air when they'd lifted the trophy. They gatecrashed Sarina Wiegman's media conference and danced on the table, informing the world that, in case we were in any doubt, it was coming home. They were ferried back to the Lensbury and partied the night away with their families and loved ones.

As for us, we washed up in a deadbeat pub somewhere in the wilder reaches of north London, but I suspect the scenes there and in the Lensbury weren't that different. The next day the Lionesses took their hangovers to Trafalgar Square. I caught a glimpse as I scooted past on a bus on my way to have lunch with a friend who worked at The FA. We sat by the river and ordered more expensively from the menu than we normally would. 'Can you believe it?' I asked her. 'No!' she replied.

Back in Trafalgar Square Rachel Daly looked like this was the platform she'd really wanted all along as she belted out 'River Deep, Mountain High', and Jill Scott interviewed the trophy. Oh, they deserved their party. In one post-match interview, Leah Williamson said they were '23 girls who would have done absolutely anything for each other'. The unbreakable unity in this team, which had become increasingly apparent throughout the tournament, and their ability to create something greater than the sum of their individual parts, was one of the major reasons why they ended up partying with the nation in Trafalgar Square.

The Lionesses had always been clear about their purpose: to inspire the nation. They didn't pass up the opportunity of the nation's attention being on their party: Ella Toone called for the huge crowds of the summer to go and watch their local teams, and the next day the Lionesses wrote to the two prime ministerial candidates. Winning the Euros, they wrote, was only the beginning. They wanted to create real change and they set out a clear aim: that every young girl in the country should be able to play football at school. 'We were often stopped from playing. So we made our own teams,' they said. I too had had to set up my own teams and I'm in full agreement with them: never again. With still just 63 per cent of girls being able to play football in PE, we have hard work on a national scale to undertake. But we must do it. Currently, whether children have access to sport – and the kind of sport they have access to – depends to a large extent on their gender. Is that what we want for our kids?

* * *

'The football is officially going on for ever.'

This is the punchline of a sketch by the comedy double act Mitchell and Webb, which on occasion used to reduce me to hysteria – not hysterical laughter but hysteria – when I was battling with the fixture list or the transfer window, and the whole shebang seemed like some millennia-long saga that just rolled on and on without end.

We'd hardly caught our breath from the Euros final when The FA announced, and immediately sold out, a Lionesses' game against the USA at Wembley. Before that, the UEFA Women's Champions League started on 21 August, only three weeks after the Euros final. Alex Greenwood, who had been one of England's remarkable substitutes in the Euros, said that some players had only had six days off.

International games resumed in early September with the small matter of qualification for the 2023 World Cup to secure. We were never to see again the team that had won the Euros. Ellen White and Jill Scott both announced their retirements, and both would see out the year on a high: Ellen announced her pregnancy, and Jill won *I'm A Celebrity … Get Me Out of Here!*

CHAPTER 4

In their first game after the Euros, the Lionesses beat Austria 2-0 on 3 September. The result meant they would definitely be going to Australia and New Zealand for the World Cup. They then played Luxembourg on 6 September in Stoke-on-Trent. I hotfooted it to Stoke, delighted that The FA were continuing to take football to fans around the country, not just in London.

Like Sunderland, Stoke is one of those cities that many people don't think is worth a visit. How wrong they are. I've now been many times and I love the place. A bequest of Charlotte Rhead pottery from a great-aunt led me to develop a massive ceramics obsession, and a day that combines a Lionesses game with a trip to the factory shops of the Stoke pottery manufacturers is how I would like every day of the afterlife to be.

My pots duly bought, I trotted off to the bet365 Stadium. It was full, loud and joyous as we watched a rampant Lionesses team beat Luxembourg 10-0. I caught up with some friends from The FA and asked them the question I was asking everyone: 'Has it sunk in yet?' It hadn't. It was to take a while for all of us.

Early September should have seen the start of the Barclays Women's Super League. The opening weekend had been set up as a showcase, designed as the perfect follow-up to the glorious summer, a 'come hither' to encourage people who'd fallen in love with the women's game to watch its elite club edition. But it wasn't to be. When Queen Elizabeth II died on 8 September, the clear mood of the country was that we should undertake national commemoration and thanksgiving with all proper honours. I wholeheartedly agreed with this. The decision was made to postpone all football. As a former CEO, I'm all too familiar with the kind of situation where there isn't a good option and you have to do the least-bad thing, so those who made the decision have my full empathy. But in my opinion, it was wrong to postpone the start of the Barclays Women's Super League. I cannot see how there was any question that playing the elite women's league after the summer we had had would present any risk of disrespect to the late Queen.

The top two women's leagues eventually kicked off later in September. By late November,

Women's Super League attendances were up 205 per cent and Women's Championship 86 per cent compared to the previous season. Some of the crowds for individual games were huge: over 40,000 at the Emirates for Arsenal v Manchester United, and over 38,000 at Stamford Bridge for Chelsea v Spurs. It was therefore no surprise when Arsenal CEO Vinai Venkatesham said in November that the club's long-term ambition was to host all Arsenal women's games at the Emirates.

England rolled on, and in October I went back to Wembley for the first time since the final, this time to see the Lionesses play the friendly against the USA that had been announced just after the Euros. The Americans were fresh from winning the CONCACAF Women's Championship (the equivalent of the Euros in North and Central America and the Caribbean). Being in a sold-out Wembley that night for another huge Lionesses game was another homecoming. These big matches tend to have a subsidiary circus around them of conferences, meet-ups, summits and the like, and this was no exception. In the posh seats, the entire women's football establishments of perhaps its two leading countries were present

The USA had for decades been the dominant women's football nation, as I had so sharply experienced way back in 1985. But now it was having its supremacy threatened by England. I sensed that the interest of many of our American sisters was not just related to matters on the pitch, but that they had smelled the whiff of commercial opportunities here in the old country. The discussions, the gossip, the fact-finding, the circling of each other a little bit were all something else. These teams had met before, and the high-ups from both English and American women's football have met before, but this time the scale of the encounter seemed bigger and with more at stake. I couldn't help but feel that the Women's Super League here and the National Women's Soccer League in the USA were about to enter an arms race to see which would become the biggest, most successful league in the world.

However, the game was overshadowed by the horrors that had been unveiled with the United States Soccer Federation's publication earlier that week of the Yates report. Sally Yates, a former deputy US Attorney General, had carried out an independent investigation into verbal and emotional abuse of players, and sexual misconduct against them, in the NWSL. Her findings were devastating. She found that the abuse had spanned multiple teams, coaches and victims. It had become 'systemic'. Player after player told Yates and her inquiry team of 'relentless, degrading tirades, manipulation that was about power, not improving performance', and 'retaliation against those who attempted to come forward'. Then there was the sexual abuse. Yates received appalling accounts from players of 'sexually charged comments, unwanted sexual advances and sexual touching, and coercive sexual intercourse.'

It went on for years during which, according to Yates, the NWSL, and the USSF, which largely controlled the NWSL, failed to have in place basic player safeguards. When they got reports from players of the misconduct, they either minimised or ignored those reports. When teams did terminate the contracts of offending coaches, they would hide the reasons for the termination, leaving the individual free to coach elsewhere. As with Hollywood and #MeToo, an entire industry stood condemned. An entire generation of girls and women had been betrayed. 'You knew', was the cry, because the authorities had known. Their wilful blindness was astounding.

Out on the pitch, the England and USA teams lined up in solidarity behind a banner saying 'Protect the Players'. National differences seemed unimportant at that moment. We are all women before we are Englishwomen or American women, and we know. We just know.

But football matches must kick off, and this one did, with both sides playing the match wholeheartedly. They wanted to give the full crowd of Wembley, and everyone watching on television, a proper match. So, while the result wasn't the main event in light of the Yates report, it's important to note that England won 2-1. The victory felt iconic given the stature of the United States women's national team, and the fact that the Lionesses had been beaten by them in the 2019 World Cup semi-final.

Were England the best team in the world? Could it be on? Were we – whisper it – in with a chance of winning the World Cup in 2023? Well, let's not be too hasty. After the defeat at Wembley, the USA went on to be beaten in friendlies by Germany and by a Spanish team missing many of its best players following the protests by 15 Spanish squad members.

England's results in friendlies across the rest of 2022 resulted in a win against Japan and two draws against the Czech Republic and Norway. Sarina Wiegman tried out new players, of course. It was difficult to read the runes of these results and predict with confidence what would happen in Australia and New Zealand, but I was entirely confident that no one was better than Sarina at putting together a championship-winning side.

* * *

Early October found me at another meeting of various people connected with women's football. The mood was convivial and the sense of optimism palpable. Again, I asked a few people the question I was asking everyone that autumn: has it sunk in yet? And most people replied that it hadn't. I don't think this was just because of the relentless cycle of football with the new season inexorably following the old season and demanding our attention. I think it's because of the enormity of what had happened. But what we were all clear about was the scale of the change that was now possible, and the sense of momentum. Things would never quite be the same again.

As for me, throughout August and September I felt pleased of course, but also fairly dispassionate about the Euros win. I too was waiting for it to hit me, which it did suddenly one day in mid-October. There wasn't a strong trigger; I just suddenly thought *We won the Euros*, and promptly cried my eyes out for the next 15 minutes.

To assist with building a strong future, the government appointed former England player Karen Carney MBE to lead a review into the future of women's football. Her remit was to convene expertise from across the game and try to super-charge its growth. Carney was an excellent choice. She's smart, no-nonsense in her approach, and ambitious for the game. She was given a wide-ranging remit covering audience reach and growth, financial health and sustainability, and structures within the game. Supported by staff from The FA and from the Department for Digital, Culture, Media & Sport, she launched a public call for evidence and brought together expert groups to consider each of the topics. Full disclosure: in early 2023 I was asked to join the expert panel she convened to help drive this vital work forward.

The work of Carney and her team ran side by side with the strategic work being undertaken by The FA and the clubs of the WSL and Women's Championship. They were looking at huge questions about the future of the league – who should own it (clubs or FA), and how it should grow. Listening to WSL/Women's Championship chair Dawn Airey give talks over the autumn, it was clear that she and her colleagues grasped the size of the opportunity and had the right level of ambition to seize it. I liked much of what I heard: set the rate of growth wisely, consider carefully where to get the necessary funds, have a clear investment strategy that ensures that all clubs and the wider ecosystem benefit.

This included plans for the two top women's leagues to leave The FA and be housed under the umbrella of a new company, with one option for it to be majority-owned by its member clubs, just as the Premier League and EFL are. The desire of clubs to control their own destiny is understandable. They are the engine rooms of the game. They develop the players, week in, week out they provide the spectacle that millions love so much. The Premier League with its 20 club members – one member, one vote – is a stellar example of how effective it is when clubs run the league they play in. And yet, I couldn't help but feel The FA had done a sterling job in building the Women's Super League and the Women's Championship to their current level. Whatever happens to the league in the future, defining its relationship with The FA and making sure it's a strong one will be critical, as will ensuring the clubs pull together for the greater good.

5

HOW DO we nourish and build our game? Men's football provides plenty of precedents, many of them excellent, but we also have the chance to build women's football to be something different with its own identity, its own triumphs. Whatever we do, we must ensure that the player is front and centre. Her welfare is paramount, her voice must be heard. We celebrate female players for freeing themselves – and, by extension, all of us – from the male gaze, but elite sport can put a different, and equally intolerable, kind of pressure on the female player's relationship with her body.

All through July 2022, there was an elephant in the room. A study released just before the start of the Euros and undertaken by academics at Central Lancashire, Loughborough and John Moores Universities gave us some devastating facts. The academics had surveyed 115 players across the Women's Super League and Women's Championship. A third of those who replied displayed eating disorder symptoms, 11 per cent reported moderate to severe anxiety summations, and 11 per cent moderate to severe depression symptoms.

This is elite football causing misery. Nothing merits or justifies it. Let's get this straight right now: women have body fat. We have more of it than men. Our body fat's a beautiful thing. While elite sport of course involves training to achieve peak playing performance, I want my football to showcase women and their bodies within healthy boundaries of female physical potential.

The men's elite game has done a decent job of building player welfare mechanisms. In 2017, in response to allegations of bullying in several sports, and historical child sexual abuse in male football, Dame Tanni Grey-Thompson was tasked with drawing up recommendations for how sport can fully exercise its duty of care to athletes, to ensure that everyone can engage with sport in a safe way. Dame Tanni commended the Premier League for taking every recommendation from her report and did something with it.

So we have a precedent. And we have no reason why this safeguarding and protection of players – and of staff too – shouldn't be the first line of our strategy.

In case we need more encouragement, we can remind ourselves of what happened in the USA: the years of systemic verbal and emotional abuse and sexual misconduct uncovered by the Yates report spanning many teams, coaches and victims. We can remind ourselves of the abuse of women footballers in other countries. We can remind ourselves of the almost wilful blindness of systems that allowed this to happen and provided no effective means to stop it happening.

And then we can ponder whether the abuse of women footballers and the systemic crushing of the ability to call time on it happen elsewhere. Lindsey Horan, the US midfielder who plays in

Europe, certainly thought so: 'This is all over the world. Being a player in Europe right now, I know that.' We like to think that we have good systems to protect players and give them a voice – and let's hope we do, but we must be forever vigilant.

Player care extends beyond sexual integrity and mental health. Our ignorance of the interplay between female physiology and elite sporting performance is astonishing. While it was wonderful that Beth Mead, Sarina Wiegman and the Lionesses effected a clean sweep of BBC Sports Personality of the Year, Coach of the Year and Team of the Year at the end of 2022, the sight of Beth and her partner and Arsenal team-mate Vivianne Miedema – another of the world's top players – attending the ceremony on crutches was heartbreaking. Both had ruptured their anterior cruciate ligaments. Female footballers are up to six times more susceptible to this knee injury than men, and we still really don't know why. Some suspect a connection between this extraordinary rate of ACL injuries among women footballers and the menstrual cycle – but we still don't really know a lot about the impact of the menstrual cycle on sporting performance either. At least teams are now turning away from making teams play in white shorts. When England captain Leah Williamson revealed at the end of the year that she suffers from endometriosis, I had no idea how she coped practically, physically or emotionally.

Then there's feet. Our feet aren't just smaller versions of men's feet. Men's feet are comparatively longer and wider, and women generally have higher malleoli (the bony bits on each side of the ankle) and higher arches. Yet I can find only one current producer of football boots – Australian manufacturer Ida – who says they have designed their boots with the specific biomechanics of the female foot in mind. What are the consequences of women wearing football boots designed for the different feet of men? You guessed it, we don't know yet.

Next on our list is ensuring that we make good on what the Lionesses asked for as their legacy: that every girl should be able to play football.

Some of the young girls of today will grow up to be the Lionesses of the future, but many of them will also grow up to be the women like me of the future: they'll never play for England but they'll be in love with football for ever. Maybe they'll work in the game in some capacity. For that to happen, we need to make sure they have access to this glorious, life-enhancing sport when they're young.

We're starting on the back foot. According to the Youth Sport Trust's 2022 annual report, the amount of PE in secondary schools has fallen by 13 per cent since 2011. When it comes to football, only 44 per cent of secondary schools provide equal football lessons for girls and boys. It's going to take determined political will and an expansion of resources to get us to where we need to be: think of all the football pitches you see around you in your town, or from your car, or whenever you take a train journey. Now double their number. Then make sure those pitches are in good condition and are not prohibitively expensive to book. Expansion of the game to the other half of the population is going to have to look something like that.

The same is true of coaches: we need many more, not just in schools but in grassroots clubs and in the Emerging Talent Centres, the elite training programmes for talented girls. And we need to make sure that girls can get to those programmes.

On 22 July 2022, 60 licences for Emerging Talent Centres, funded by the Premier League and regulated by The FA, were awarded. By the end of the 2023/24 season, over 4,200 girls will be involved in these centres – more than double the current number. This is welcome and will also help with another much-discussed issue about the Lionesses: the lack of ethnic diversity in the team that won the Euros. An England team drawn from a narrow demographic will deter girls from certain groups from thinking that football is for them. This is not to take away from the Lionesses and the clubs that have developed them, but we want *all* little girls – whatever their ethnicity and wherever their home and whatever their socio-economic background – to be able to look to the national team and see versions of themselves providing the inspiration to believe that football is for them.

Consider the following list: Nottingham, Berwick-upon-Tweed, Chesterfield, Milton Keynes, Harrogate, Barrow-in-Furness, Rochdale, Whitby, Reading, North Walsham and Aylesbury. These are the birthplaces of the 11 players who started for the Lionesses in every Euros game. London, Manchester and Birmingham – cities that with their surrounding conurbations collectively account for 26 per cent of the population of England – are entirely missing from the list. If our national team was mirroring our national population, we should be seeing three or so players from these cities in the England starting line-up. In the Euros, we had none. Each of these cities also has more residents identifying as belonging to the Asian, Black, Mixed or Other ethnic groups than the English average. The lack of ethnic diversity isn't exclusively caused by the lack of big-city representation but there's a connection.

Admittedly, when we look at the data from the wider squad, we see a couple of players from our big cities: some of them came on as subs and made huge contributions. Two of them – Chloe Kelly and Ella

Toone – scored the goals in the final. Nevertheless, we have work to do. We need to understand why talented young girls in our big cities have been failed. Some clubs in cities got it right: as noted earlier, Sunderland AFC were a superstar of elite female football development. We need to look at success stories like Sunderland to see what lessons can be learned from them.

We're now seeing greater investment in girls' and women's football by all professional clubs, which is to be welcomed. Investment such as this, together with programmes such as Discover My Talent run by The FA and the EFL Trust, and the expansion of the Emerging Talent Centre programme, should all help. But it's not as simple as 'if you build it, they will come'. The girls also have to get there. The Academy of Light, Sunderland AFC's elite training centre, is the most beautiful place I have ever worked. Herons dipped for fish in the reed beds that recycled the site's water. When the players had gone for the day, hares would bound across the pitches, and I used to have arguments with the groundsman about whether he *really* needed to mow the scarlet pimpernel and oxeye daisies that bloomed in the verges (he did – their seedlings could ruin the pitches).

Having been built out of town, Sunderland's is typical of most academies. It's hard to find an inner-city, brownfield site of sufficient size for an academy (although Manchester City did). If you're Sunderland, you can find a greenfield site three miles out of town. If you're a London club, it's more likely to be 20 miles. Wherever it is, there may well be access difficulties, particularly as greenfield sites tend to be more poorly served by public transport. Reliance on parents' ability to ferry girls to training is not an option for those families without a car, or those parents working two or even three jobs to keep the show on the road, or with caring responsibilities for other children in the family. In the elite boys' game, while there has been more resource available to bring the children to the football, it can be an issue also.

Aston Villa may be showing the way forward. Glorious Warwickshire countryside surrounds their main academy at Bodymoor Heath, but Villa are also coming back into Birmingham, with an additional inner-city academy – to be used by both the boys' and the girls' set-ups – currently being built near Villa Park.

We have to either take the children to the football or the football to the children. Maybe we have to compensate parents for taking time out to support their footballing child. However we do it, we need to make sure nobody's left out.

Next, we need to understand and take down other barriers that can prevent girls from particular demographics from playing and being able to reach their full potential. Britons of Asian heritage – nearly 10 per cent of the English population – are hugely under-represented in both male and female elite football. In April 2022, the Premier League and anti-racism football charity Kick It Out launched an action plan to identify talented boys of South Asian heritage and increase the number of them within our academies. It's an innovative and much-needed project, and it should be followed closely by those tasked with building the girls' talent pipeline.

Then, once the children are at football, they need to be made to feel welcome, valued and safe. Black women tell stories of girls being discriminated against in grassroots football because of their hair or because of nebulous reasons such as 'being not the right fit'. This kind of discrimination can happen in the elite game too: I spoke to an elite player who remains on anti-depressants due to her earlier experiences in football. In her time in the game, she told me that she'd had team-mates talk about her 'super noodle' (i.e. Black) hair. At one club, she was called a 'monkey' and told to 'go and join your gang' (of other Black players) and was also sexually abused. In an echo of what the Yates report uncovered in the USA, she didn't say anything for months, becoming more and more stressed and withdrawn. The reason? 'Players who face racial abuse are in a precarious position,' she told me. If they speak up, will the system protect them or will it further isolate and traumatise them?

She'd had good experiences too: she spoke fondly of one club that was wholly supportive and welcoming. Critically, that club had a diverse squad and coaching staff. When I asked her what needed to change so that every club was like that, she replied 'everything'.

How do we break down that 'everything'? She told me that the way Black players are treated and represented needs to change and that diversity in senior coaching, administration and leadership needs to be radically improved. We must ensure that the system we create doesn't isolate and further traumatise those who have experienced trauma. And we must ensure that all levels of the system are open to all – that English football's players, workforce and leadership look like the population of England.

The eradication of systemic bias is hard work but it's vital work. Without it, I fear we may still be having the same conversations about lack of diversity and about access barriers within the women's game in 20 years' time. Let's not let that happen.

* * *

As we've seen, WSL crowds grew after the Euros, and while there were some headline-grabbing attendances, most crowds were still small. Spurs play most of their games at Brisbane Road, where their crowds hover around the 2,000 mark. Leicester City play all their games at the King Power Stadium (capacity 32,261) but up to the end of November 2022 they only broke the 4,000 barrier once.

Stadiums are critical to the growth of a league. It was arguably the rebuilding and renewing of our stadiums after the Hillsborough disaster that kicked off the growth of the Premier League: create modern, comfortable, iconic stadia like the Stadium of Light to replace romantic old dumps like Roker Park, and more people will come, even despite the fact – as in Sunderland's case – the football has never been of a Premier League-winning standard.

A stadium is a kind of home. Obviously, it's the home of the team, but to many fans it's a place of emotional significance and safety. Their club's stadium has familiarity. It has memories. It's a venue for the celebration and strengthening of ties of kinship and community. I used to think that women's football was going to need a whole raft of new stadia around the country, each of 10–15,000 capacity, and each built to Premier League standards of spectator comfort, pitch protection and broadcasting facilities. While I've no doubt that this is what some clubs need, I'm no longer so sure there is one model that fits all. Some teams may be able to play at the main stadium, as Arsenal would love to do, or they may need to build a new ground. Each club will need to find its own solution to what looks like 'home' for its women's team, but I would like to see solutions that deliver stadia that will be iconic and forever identified with the women's team – stadia where fans can accrue memories and history year by year.

Once clubs have got their stadium, they have to encourage big, passionate and partisan crowds. This passion looks great on TV and it's what sells football to broadcasters. Those broadcasters are knocking on an open door: there's a new breed of women's football fan. My cousin Helen is typical. Her husband Malcolm is football-mad and over the years she's joined him to an extent, although never with his full passion, in following the vicissitudes of his beloved Norwich City. Unlike me, though, Helen wasn't brought up with football and before the Euros she probably wouldn't have called herself a fan. When the tournament kicked off, she thought she'd 'show willing' by watching it when it was on TV.

Her conversion was fast and absolute, and she told me it was because of the sheer joy of it. She recognised the players' artistry and effort; she loved how England played as a team and unselfishly; she began to appreciate the moves that were being made, the instinct for knowing a player would run into space, and what she described to me as 'those ziggy-zaggy things they do' (no, me neither). Before too long she couldn't wait for the next match – and not just England's games. To her husband's amusement, she started insisting they got home for kick-offs. To her own amusement and astonishment, when she bumped into a girlfriend one day they immediately started talking about football. After the semi-final she texted me, 'If only your dad could see this.' If only indeed.

And she kept coming back to that word 'joy'. The joy of the crazy 8-0 against Norway. The joy of the spontaneity and freedom with which the Lionesses played. The joy of the Lionesses dancing on the table at the media conference after the final. The joy of watching the matches on TV on hot summer days with the windows open, and hearing the cheers from all the neighbours' houses at England's goals.

This is how we win fans – through quality football that entertains, brings delight, and weaves compelling narratives on and off the pitch – but it's not all that's needed to retain a crowd. Although the opening fixtures of the WSL season gave us some shocks, after eight matches we'd settled into business as usual. Three of the top four WSL clubs were the same as three of the top four Premier League clubs. The top WSL team had 21 points from a maximum 24 and the bottom team had none.

Crowds won't come if they already know the score. Healthy and vibrant leagues must have jeopardy. It must be possible for a WSL team to achieve the equivalent of Leicester City winning the Premier League. That Leicester City win was not an accident; it's built into the design of the Premier League with its relatively flat distribution of central revenue between top and bottom clubs. Of course, Leicester City winning the Premier League is the exception not the rule, but it's far from impossible that we'll see its like again.

How resource is not only raised but distributed has to be a central consideration as the WSL and Women's Championship grow. Money and expertise need to be focused onto the lower end of the Women's Super League, and onto the Women's Championship, in order to build the capacity and performance of all teams. This sounds easy, but the WSL's business model – just like the Premier League's – is predicated on the best talent in the world playing in the league. The top teams will increasingly compete in an international market for the most gifted players, just as the men's teams do. They will understandably cry foul if, as central revenue grows, a flat distribution model and spending controls mean they are outgunned for talent by Spain's Barcelona, France's Olympique Lyonnais or the USA's Angel City.

There's a constant tension in a league. The top clubs drive much of the central commercial value; the lower-placed clubs not only need to be there (otherwise it's not a league) but they need to have the chance to grow and thrive: winning the damn thing must always be a possibility that can be striven for with effort and time. The Premier League has managed to hold the line between individual club growth and collective league growth for 30 years with great success (including seeing off the occasional attempt at disruption such as the European Super League). The WSL and Women's Championship must do likewise.

There are, however, elements of governance where women's football should not just match men's football but do better. When it comes to the question of who should run women's football, my answer is unequivocal: the people who are best qualified to do so. However, women have a unique moral ownership of women's football. The day must never come when women are as under-represented in the leadership of women's football as they are in the leadership of men's football. The football bodies should set a vision now for what the workforce of women's football – in all roles and at all levels of seniority – should look like. As I've already said, this isn't complicated: the football workforce in all roles and at all levels of seniority should look like the population of England. This is not just a matter of sentiment or social justice warriorship. It's a matter of good business: diverse teams deliver better results. And if this is right for women's football, surely it must be right for men's football too.

The dominant model of team ownership and management within England's highest two leagues is that of the women's team sitting within a big professional men's club. There are notable and worthy exceptions in the Women's Championship but not in the Women's Super League. The support and investment that many professional men's clubs give to their women's teams is impressive. I was eyewitness to one example when I went to the opening of Brighton & Hove Albion FC's new £8.5m women's and girls' training facility in late August 2022. It's magnificent.

But being part of a larger male club is not without risks. The first is that the fate of the women's team will simply shadow that of the men's team. As we have seen, this means that the top of the WSL can echo the top of the Premier League: a rich men's team flush with revenue from the UEFA Champions League, from wealthy owners, and from being a global brand will find it much easier to fund its women's team to triumph. This isn't to say they will find it easy – they still have to do all the difficult things that need to be done to make a football team successful – but they are more likely to be able to find the necessary resource to do it. If a men's team fails, however, the women's set-up can be seen as a 'soft' area of spending, one of the first cost centres to be cut.

How do we ring-fence women's teams from this? The real answer is to make them self-sufficient entities that can play and trade on their own terms, but we are still some years off that being realistic. The FA have set a target date of 2032 for the women's game becoming self-sustaining. I'm going to make a prediction (perhaps emboldened by my predictions of 30 years ago that the Lionesses could win the Euros and Barclays could sponsor the WSL) that I think it'll happen before then, say by 2028.

One option may be to require any funding from a parent men's team to be given – and, critically, secured in escrow – for three seasons forward on a rolling basis. If in those three seasons the men's team fails to meet any of its playing and hence financial targets – if it fails to qualify for the UEFA Champions League, for example, or if it gets relegated – it simply can't claw that money back. Likewise, we need to plan now for when women's football starts to break even. We need to start talking now about how much of the profit that women's football will eventually generate can and should be ploughed back into the men's game.

Towards the close of 2022, the England men's team left the World Cup at the quarter-final stage, but they left it with every reason to hold their heads high. As fans, we were gutted, but there was much to be hopeful about with this team. There was outstanding young talent breaking through. There were good performances. After the men's Euros in

2021, a friend in the game said to me 'Have you noticed how nice footballers now are?' He made a good point: this England men's team were humble, grounded and genuine while also being dedicated and superb professionals. It felt like England players had come a long way from the days when one nearly crashed his car while yelling 'they're taking the piss!' because a club had 'only' offered him £55,000 a week.

After the men's team's defeat to France in the World Cup quarter-final, the official Lionesses' account tweeted 'Family' and the broken-heart emoji. I thought of Harry Maguire going to Lionesses' Euros games, of Jordan Henderson walking into training at Liverpool with an England shirt with 'Williamson' on the back, and of how senior players on both teams had championed issues affecting those far less fortunate than them. Of course, there are highly skilled PR and media professionals working across the England set-ups, yet I couldn't help but feel we were seeing a new type of England: inclusive, connected, and one where the women stood shoulder to shoulder with the men. It all hit exactly the right note. It was what it should be.

And then there's our girls and young women. I think back to 13-year-old Alice Ritson, who I'd met with her family at the Euros final. When I spoke to her after the game, she told me her dream was to be a Lioness, but not just any Lioness – she wanted to be like Alex Scott or Ella Toone and score lots of goals. Or her 20-year-old sister Annabel, who selflessly stopped playing in order to focus on coaching the girls' team that she'd led for years when it became clear she couldn't do both in the time available to her. Her dream was simple: for there to be more women's and girls' football in her club and all around the North-East of England. Their dad Paul beamed with pride at the pair of them, and I don't blame him for one single second.

There are thousands of girls and young women like Alice and Annabel all across the country: they're playing football, they're helping others to play football, and they're dreaming enormous, beautiful football dreams.

CHAPTER 5

Haway the lasses. Haway the lads. Haway England.

* * *

What about me, pilgrim along football's path for half a century now? The football deities had an enormous and delightful shock in store for me. It began when I was at the Equal Playing Field conference about gender equality in football in the week before the Euros final. A woman I didn't know came up to me and said she was setting up a recreational football team for women over 30. Would Women in Football be interested in covering the story? 'Why yes,' I said, 'it's the kind of story we love. Let me hook you up with our Comms Manager. Oh, by the way, where is it?' In reply she named a small community centre that is a mere five minutes' walk from the bench by the level crossing on the way to the supermarket.

Well, how about that.

So since September 2022 I have been doing what I thought I would never do again: I am playing football. Our little set-up is part of the new wave of recreational football opportunities for women and girls springing up like snowdrops nodding their elegant heads out of the hard ground after a long winter. For the first two weeks, I walked there in tears and I walked back in tears because this game – this extraordinary, magnificent game – is nothing if you don't play it, and because I never thought I would be able to play again, and because mine is the last generation of women who will have to wait decades to do so. I am beyond grateful to J and S, who have set it up and got the funding for it, and to H and B, our coaches.

H and B are in their early twenties, play part-time and also coach. They are wonderful coaches and their work with us has brought utter joy to my life. The future of women's football is in their hands and in the hands of women like them – and, having got to know these two, I can say that it's going to be in very safe hands. Currently they are players and coaches, two of the most important roles in the game. But down the line, who knows how and where their football careers will take them?

Wherever it is, Women in Football will be there to support and champion them.

For now, H and B have on their hands a team of middle-aged lady beginners and re-starters like me who have not played for decades. We do our dribbling drills and our passing drills and we play in mini-games. It's the first time in my life that I have been properly coached.

It has had knock-on effects as well. I discovered that my heart and lung fitness wasn't as good as it needed to be for the explosive nature of football, so I restarted Couch to 5k. I built a few yoga stretches into my daily routine. Public policy managers take note: football is a gateway sport and if you fund a bunch of women to play it once a week, the chances are they'll do other physical activity too.

But here's the thing: the ball and I – well, it has begun to feel like dancing, which it never did first time round. I have begun to have a little go at shimmying, misleading, even turning like Alessia Russo for her second goal against Northern Ireland. It's heaven. It rarely comes off, and I remain a not very good footballer, but I feel like I'm in lockstep with this little sphere of magic at my feet as we build our relationship. I watch it as it dances about, I try to make tiny adjustments to my kick so it stays under control. I haven't cracked this yet, and perhaps I never well, but it's bliss trying.

What a turn-up in my football journey. At a time in life when people begin to think more about things ending (as I do, and not in a morbid way, it's natural), I have had the great fortune to have a new and wonderful beginning, or rather a return to something.

I think back to my childhood, when my brother would disappear immediately after breakfast to play football all day with his friends, only returning when it was time for tea. Back then, girls – bar a handful of brilliant and wonderful pioneers – simply didn't do that. If someone said to me now, 'Jane, come and play football all day,' I'd go like a shot. It feels like a part of childhood I should have had but didn't – and it's not too late to put that right. So if you see a woman in her late fifties kicking a ball round a park, don't laugh at her. It might be me.

'Thirty years of hurt,' says the famous song. My banishment from playing football has finally ended after nearly 30 long years. The time from the English ban to the English triumph at the Euros was 100 years. But bans, sexism, debilitating cultural assumptions about sport and gender never stopped thousands of us dreaming. Football is finally home, and as I go to a sports shop to buy my second-ever pair of football boots, 37 years after I bought my first pair, I'm overwhelmed by emotion. Part of the emotion is utter love of this magical game. But part of it is the realisation that football's not the only one who's come home.

I'm home too.

ABOUT THE AUTHOR

JANE PURDON qualified as a solicitor in 1994, and joined Sunderland AFC as club secretary and solicitor in 2001. There she undertook the full range of legal work of a leading club, and hers was one of the first such appointments by a Premier League club.

In 2005, she joined the Premier League, rising to become director of governance in 2011. While at the Premier League, Jane drafted the first iteration of the Youth Development Rules, which gave effect to the Elite Player Performance Plan, the new blueprint for elite talent development in English football.

In 2015, Jane moved to UK Sport as head of governance and leadership, where she co-authored the first edition of the Code for Sports Governance. In 2018, she became the first-ever CEO of Women in Football, the world's leading organisation to support, champion and celebrate women in the game. She stood down in 2021 but remains on the board. In addition, she chairs the board of the Professional Game Academy Audit Company, the independent auditor and quality-assurance body of all academies in the male professional game.

Jane also lectures extensively on sport business and governance, and undertakes executive coaching with the leaders and future leaders of the game. In 2022, she was awarded a Master of Fine Arts in Creative Writing with Distinction from Manchester Metropolitan University.